WHERE WAS YOUR *Wrath* WHEN WE NEEDED IT?

ANGELA DI PARADISO

"Freedom is never more than one generation away from extinction. We didn't pass it to our children in the bloodstream. It must be fought for, protected, and handed-on for them to do the same, or one day we will spend our sunset years telling our children and our children's children what it was once like in the United States where men were free."
-Ronald Reagan

It is 2036, and things that prior generations had taken for granted had dramatically changed over the past dozen years, and not for the better. No one could have imagined the world as it had become, except for the elitist members of the NEW WORLD ORDER who had planned it, going back to the late 1700s when the organization known as the BAVARIAN ILLUMINATI imagined the elimination of individual countries and governments in favor of their vision of an ILLUMINATI-controlled, one-world government enterprise.

Their secretive and devious plans had always been vulnerable to public exposure and challenge, but the ILLUMINATI were not just a small, insignificant group of conspiratorial cultists. They were of significant intellectual prowess and financial superiority to the common man, and their rise was reflective of their social and political influence.

As a result, they continually gained global support in spite of numerous attempts to disclose their sinister plans, as their control of media, coupled with the interference by well-positioned inductees, was instrumental in the deflection and derailment of the fortuitous warnings of their very existence. The most relevant warning came from George Orwell, in his book, <u>1984</u>, which stated, "The Party told you to reject the evidence of your eyes and ears. It was their final, most essential command." As was the greatest part of their deception, they were masters of propaganda, successfully dismissing Orwell's warning as a fantastical work of fiction.

Consequently, centuries-long governmental and societal ignorance made their plan succeed, eventually paving the way for significant displays of power and influence in the 20th Century, to a full-scale destruction of the United States of America in the 21st Century. In the presidential election of 2024, the citizens of the United States of America allowed the NEW WORLD ORDER to make its final assault to eliminate the first line of global defense for human rights and protection of freedom from totalitarianism with the installation of their newest disciple as President. Without delay the NEW WORLD ORDER implemented the centuries-long plannings of their take-over, as Americans helplessly witnessed and suffered the effects of being the first domino to fall under the control of the NEW WORLD ORDER.

Regrettably, it didn't take long for all to recognize that when the first domino falls, eventually, they all fall.

The drive on "The 5" freeway in California had not changed much in Chelsea's lifetime. The ocean view and all its glory had always been on full display from San Diego to Dana Point, where "The 5" veers to the east and eventually ends up in the middle of the state for the remainder of its northern pursuit, all the way to the Canadian border in Washington State. Once upon a time, meaning pre-2029, Chelsea, instead of subjecting herself to the endless boredom of bumper-to-bumper big rigs and farmland landscapes on both sides of "The 5", had always made the transition to "The 101" at its southern terminus in the heart of the City of Los Angeles for the remainder of the drive to visit family and the home she grew up in, in Sonoma. As a history teacher, "The 101" had a great backstory for her, as much of "The

101" follows the original El Camino Real, translated to be The King's Highway, which was the route used by Spanish missionaries to travel between the twenty-one missions they built at various locations along the route during the 1700s.

Depending on the time of day or night, from the heart of Los Angeles it was traditionally an expected ride of stop-and-go traffic, gridlock, and frustration for the next seventy miles until you got to the City of Ventura, an original El Camino Real Mission city, where "The 101" generally opened up and resumed the coastal ride all the way to San Luis Obispo. Once there, if you had a little extra time to kill, and to stay on the actual coast, you would transition to the CA 1, one of the most beautiful stretches of highway in North America.

Though not advisable while driving, Chelsea began to day-dream of what her life could have been if the current state of affairs had never developed. She had wanted to someday experience the joys of life that her parents, grandparents, and all past generations had enjoyed, but the events of the past several years made it quite apparent that it was never going to happen. The list of banned practices grew daily, as the NEW WORLD ORDER's sphere of unfettered control widened and increased in severity.

General traffic, meaning automobiles, were sparse on the freeways, as the population of the United States was now only at 40% of what it was pre-pandemic, meaning before 2029. People didn't drive anymore, or go anywhere, as unrestricted travel was no longer an unalienable right in America. Vacations were now a thing of the past, with even Disneyland, the greatest vacation destination in the free world for over seventy-five years, having been closed for seven years. All of the passenger vehicles in the country were NEW WORLD ORDER owned-and-controlled electric vehicles with systems that monitored the driver's speed and allowable travel distance. Nothing else was permitted. Even motorcycles were more like electric bicycles, meaning no one ever saw or heard them on the freeways. Lane-splitting motorcyclists would almost be welcomed at this point.

Awakening from her mental drift, Chelsea wasn't quite sure what had made her suddenly want to make this particular trip, except to get back home for the first time in four years and spend some time with her two older brothers. Since leaving home at eighteen for college, she had only gone home once a year, for Christmas, but the Pandemic of 2029 changed everything as two of the casualties of the pandemic were her mother and father. She hadn't been able to go and see their graves, located in a family plot on the property, until 2032 when the government finally lifted what in essence was Martial Law, requiring the total lockdown of the country for over three years. Though the total lockdown was no longer called Martial Law, it was the form of government that the surviving members of what was once the United States were now permanently living under.

Adhering to the on-board computer system-warning, Chelsea stopped at a car-charging station on the north end of Ventura, CA, which historically had been a laid-back beach town. The sign above the entrance clearly read Charging Station, but when the sign was installed, the NEW WORLD ORDER made no attempt to hide the ghost of the logo that had been clearly displayed on each and every charging unit in the station for over fifteen years prior. The ghost was clear enough to easily make out the original sign's name - Tesla. The reason for not totally obscuring it, was to most an admission of indifference to hide it, but it was intentional on many levels. It was there to remind people that the past was dead, and the future was now at the mercy of the NEW WORLD ORDER.

Seeing the remnants of the Tesla logo served as a constant reminder of the eerie events in early 2030 that had led to the elimination of Tesla. With the pandemic only months old, the first volley to permanently eliminate all free speech came with the arrest of Elon Musk, who still held the title of the world's richest man and owner of Tesla and X. In an early morning raid at his personal residence, Musk was handcuffed and dragged from his house by the NEW WORLD ORDER FBI in a very public display, taken to jail and charged with sedition against the United States for allowing free speech on the X platform. He was denied legal counsel and a speedy trial, all in direct violation of what was once the bedrock of laws, the US Constitution. All of his operations, on all continents, had been seized. Without explanation, Musk was never heard from again, and no one dared to even whisper the obvious - that he had been euthanized. To further the unfettered power and fear derived by and of the NEW WORLD ORDER, it was common knowledge that any whisperers or questioners would meet the same fate.

But it was much easier to do in 2030, as the election of 2024 saw Donald Trump denied the presidency for the second time, and in the same manner as the election of 2020. Never one to surrender, Donald Trump, the last vestige of hope to stop the NEW WORLD ORDER, though too old to run in 2028, was nowhere near too old to fight, and put his empire, money, and clout behind his son to get the Republican nomination. But shortly before what turned out to actually be a hoax, instead of a standard Primary Season leading up to the 2028 election, former President Donald Trump suddenly experienced the second invasion of Mar-a-Lago by the NEW WORLD ORDER FBI. Donald Trump was handcuffed, arrested, and carried off. The only explanation of his subsequent death was for the NEW WORLD ORDER FBI to announce that he had simply died in custody.

Weeks later, the entire resistance movement to the NEW WORLD ORDER also disappeared when the NEW WORLD ORDER candidate, masquerading under the banner of the Democratic National Committee, claimed victory in the presidential election. Before anyone could even hint at contesting the election, a series of early morning raids, reminiscent of the early morning raids on Republicans and Conservatives going back to the first day that the puppet of the NEW WORLD ORDER, Joe Biden, took office in 2021. Within hours of the NEW WORLD ORDER successor to Joe Biden being sworn in, the rest of the Trump family were arrested, with the NEW WORLD ORDER using the same ploy of sedition to justify the arrests. None of them were ever heard from again. Less than two months later, the Pandemic of 2029 hit. The NEW WORLD ORDER-controlled government declared Martial Law, immediately providing an unfettered path to take full control of the government and more importantly, the military. With the United States unable to defend itself from the enemy within, less powerful countries, worldwide, fell like dominos.

But the NEW WORLD ORDER wasn't done. With Musk and Trump out of the way, they set their sights on the second richest man on the planet, Jeff Bezos of Amazon, who naively thought that his politics would shield him from their clutches. He also paid the ultimate price after finding out that Amazon itself was a threat to the NEW WORLD ORDER, as it represented all that the NEW WORLD ORDER was against- not just capitalism, but the freedom of choice. The same-style early morning raid and arrest saw Bezos also disappear forever, and his entire empire confiscated by the NEW WORLD ORDER. It became readily clear to everyone that the NEW WORLD ORDER had made "good" on its promises to itself, to make the world a *living* Hell, until such time as they got around to euthanizing anyone they didn't need to keep.

The first thing Chelsea did after getting out of her car was to place her left forearm under a scanner, allowing the scanner to read the chip that had been implanted under her skin as a permanent form of identification, as without the chip the charging station wouldn't work. The chip provided her name, age, health history, and vaccination status, which was what the NEW WORLD ORDER had promised it was all it was supposed to do, in order to protect her from catching or spreading a virus. It became mandatory in much of the free world to have the implant, as the pandemic of 2029 had caused the death of over 100 million in the United States, and unquestionably over two billion people, worldwide, which was short of the goal of the NEW WORLD ORDER by numbers that only they knew.

What no one knew was that the pandemic was nothing more than a catalyst for getting the vaccine. People didn't die from the pandemic as it would have been too difficult to control, if it had been as contagious as the masses were led to believe. Pandemic deaths were highly exploited, though only the NEW WORLD ORDER knew that the pockets of high mortality were like controlled-burns in a forest fire. As was tested and discovered in the COVID Pandemic of 2020, the masses flocked to be vaccinated. The millions of deaths were actually the result of the vaccine, which was administered by color code to eliminate those that the NEW WORLD ORDER thought should be immediately eliminated, or saved to be used as drones, going forward.

She had just finished inserting the charging nozzle before leaning against her car to wait-out the fifteen-minute process to receive a charge that would be sufficient to travel two hundred miles. Though the technology had advanced enough to allow for an eight-hundred-mile charge, it was by design that no one be able to get a longer charge or go farther than two hundred miles. It was the NEW WORLD ORDER's way to monitor the travel of all *workers,* a name that had long-since replaced the word *citizens*, a word that once described any and all free-born Americans since before the ink had dried on the Constitution of the United States. As a matter of fact, all references and copies of the US Constitution were now forbidden since NEW WORLD ORDER had come into absolute power in 2032.

Twenty other people were also at the station, and sadly, what she observed was that all of them were unsurprisingly going about the task of charging their car in a zombie-like state of nothingness, void of interaction or contact with one another; a condition that had rapidly become the norm over the past few years. People in the United States had simply given up being nice or cordial. No one said "hell-o" to strangers, held the door for anyone, or paid attention to anyone but themselves; no comments on the weather, and no comments about how long it was taking to charge their cars. Nothing. There just wasn't any point in doing so as there was no reward for being nice to your fellow Man. It was just easier to stand silent. The average person was now living in a trance-like state of submission to the NEW WORLD ORDER, its dictates, its propaganda, and its totalitarian governance.

What they did have in common was that most would continually look at the digital screens above each charging station, all of which were displaying the same message in a loop, playing over and over, so that if one were to miss the entire message on the first loop, they were guaranteed to see it on the second or third loop, because one loop was only five minutes, and the total time needed for a charge was fifteen minutes. The screens were the conduit of propaganda with both overt and subliminal context, as a permanent solution for mind control, established by the NEW WORLD ORDER. The recurring message on this particular day, was meant to serve as a reminder of how fortunate all Americans should be that they no longer needed presidential elections, as we no longer had a President. As was its intent, the recurring messages and themes constantly reminded the masses how fortunate they were to no longer have to think for themselves or fend for themselves. The NEW WORLD ORDER was in total control and would take care of everything.

This was only the first time she had stopped to recharge since starting her journey from the detention facility that used to be known as Camp Pendleton in northern San Diego County, before it was taken over as part of the American demilitarization efforts once the NEW WORLD ORDER had seized control of the United States Government. The former Marine Corp training base, which had been an integral part of ensuring US military superiority across the globe since 1942, had been decommissioned only three years ago, and as a NEW WORLD ORDER facility was basically a commune-type housing facility for thousands, with only a small part of the former base being utilized to house the weaponry and brainwashed soldiers needed for the NEW WORLD ORDER to maintain order in the newly formed society.

Of course, the promise was for a utopian paradise for all, in which the totalitarian/oligarchy NEW WORLD ORDER would seemingly provide for everyone. There would be no need or privilege for anyone to be rich or poor, successful or non-successful, married or unmarried, and most of all, happy or sad. The NEW WORLD ORDER would make all decisions for you, and were in total control of all aspects of human existence.

At most, the hierarchy of the NEW WORLD ORDER was at about 1% of the population. They were the only ones who had any chance at being happy, with no one being certain what the measure of happiness truly was, in a totalitarian society. But for sure, the remaining 99% would end up sad and miserable, including all of the gullible and naïve drones who had done everything in their power to help the NEW WORLD ORDER take over. As for the approximate 50% that comprised the opposition forces to the NEW WORLD ORDER takeover, the seemingly strong and healthy were conscripted, quite involuntarily into slaves, or as the NEW WORLD ORDER liked to call them- *workers*. The others were summarily taken to the *Farm*.

Somewhere around the three-quarter mark of getting a full charge, she noticed a van drive to the charging station and park in front of the only entry-and-exit driveway, to prohibit anyone from coming in or leaving until they had finished scanning everyone at the charging station. No one dared complain, and at this point no one would even think about it as it was common practice to be detained in this manner. When they got to Chelsea, she, as the others had done, simply held out her arm to be scanned, but the policeman looked at her, and without so much as a word, dismissed her as if she weren't even there. She thought it odd that the policeman had not stopped to scan her, making her wonder if the newer technology was able to read her chip from afar, or even knowing she had just finished complying with a self-scan, so maybe it wasn't necessary.

By the time the policemen had left the station, allowing autos to uninterruptedly come and go again, the *message of the day* was about to start for the third time. Now that she was fully charged, she was ready to continue on her journey.

Immediately after leaving the station, just before exiting the City of Ventura, Chelsea had to stop for one of the new additions to most major roads and highways in America, which was a Checkpoint, reminiscent of the almost-forgotten checkpoint just north of Camp Pendleton. Prior to 2020, when the immigration laws were in full force and effect, every car had to stop so that the US Border and Customs officers could make a determination, based on the then-still-legal practice of profiling, to quickly assess whether or not you were transporting drugs and/or illegal aliens in your vehicle.

Now, agonizingly having to endure the stop-and-go caravan waiting for agents to scan the arm-chips of every occupant of every vehicle, Chelsea began to ruefully and angrily reminisce the events that allowed for the final assault of the NEW WORLD ORDER. It came in late 2024.

With Joe Biden having outlived his usefulness, the NEW WORLD ORDER brought in their next candidate to be President of the United States, via an unquestionably-rigged election, and let Biden drift off into a detached and disconnected state of existence, to live out his final months in a high-backed chair with a comforter over his lap, on the back porch of his home in Delaware. As a Christmas present to his family, the last official act of his presidency was pardoning his son, Hunter, and all of the Biden family members. It was an overnight transition, quite easily accomplished by simply cutting him off from the daily medications that had allowed him to even know what day it was for the entirety of his presidency, and then dismissing him with about as much fanfare as throwing out an old shirt.

With Biden and Harris out, the newest disciple of the NEW WORLD ORDER, commonly referred to as the *Closer* in quiet conversations of conservative groups, emerged as President of the United States in 2024, and immediately proceeded to drive the last handful of nails into the coffin of the United States of America. And this was easier than had been anticipated as the DEMOCRATIC PARTY, aka the NEW WORLD ORDER, had also seized control of the Congress and the Senate by the same means. In his first term, the Closer continued down the unfettered path that the Biden presidency had first-laid out after the 2020 election, with unbridled determination to implement all of the final processes, and accelerate the plan for the NEW WORLD ORDER to assume full control and total domination of the United States of America, and ultimately, the entire world.

The Pandemic of 2029 made the Covid Pandemic of 2020 look like the 24-hour flu. Because the panic of uncertainty had overcome the masses, by government decree Martial Law was instituted, forcing the United States into total lockdown at 6 pm daily. Once the country, and the world for that matter, was in lockdown, the NEW WORLD ORDER carried-out their final strategy to eliminate any chance of an armed revolt. The lockdown allowed the NEW WORLD ORDER to confiscate a majority of the guns owned by US citizens, concentrating mostly on all forms of weaponry that were of military grade ordinance. Human interaction with anyone but one's family members in your primary household was a felony and resulted in immediate arrest by the US Military, which was now the enforcement arm of the NEW WORLD ORDER government. By the end of 2030, to end all dissenting views, the US Constitution was declared illegal and the US Supreme Court was disbanded.

Over forty million Americans died in the Pandemic of 2029. By 2032 the NEW WORLD ORDER had euthanized another sixty million Americans. The Holocaust of WWII was nothing compared to the genocide committed by the NEW WORLD ORDER. Undaunted and doubling down on their efforts, in 2032 the NEW WORLD ORDER got rid of that many, again, in the first six months of seizing total control. Each and every year afterward, the old, the weak, and the sick, who offered no value to support the needed manpower to keep the NEW WORLD ORDER alive, were summarily eliminated. As was the case in WWII, the NEW WORLD ORDER was happy that all of the gas-fired energy plants across America hadn't been decommissioned yet, as they provided a ready-made series of crematoriums to quickly dispose of the remains.

As for the gullible and naïve drones who blindly followed the NEW WORLD ORDER, they too had to submit to the most menial jobs imaginable in order to provide the barest of necessities for any civilization to survive. The tens of millions who were the victims of believing that they, themselves, would reap the benefits of their undying support of the end-goals of the NEW WORLD ORDER, were the most miserable, and in the highest percentile of suicides. After all, who wants a bunch of cry-babies and potential turncoats against the NEW WORLD ORDER, just because millions of anticipants who thought their reward for blindly helping to crush the forces of GOOD would be to share in the spoils that the 1% were enjoying, didn't materialize. Whether it was vocalized to them or simply accepted by them, the message was the same: *Just shut up and do as you're told, and if you don't like it, kill yourself!!!*

Looking back, it was hard to imagine how far their control had escalated in just a few short years, and how clear it was to everyone on the planet that there was no way to reverse it. Those chances had been eliminated with the presidential election of 2024, and there was no turning back.

Before Chelsea could accelerate past twenty miles per hour, her attention was immediately drawn to a hitch-hiker standing on the side of the road, holding a small cardboard sign in his hand with a message that simply said, "North." It wasn't the sign that had actually caught her attention, but his mode of dress. His long, dark, wavy hair and neatly trimmed beard only accentuated the mystique of this man who was dressed in a long robe, tied with a rope at the waist, wearing sandals, and carrying a tall staff. But interestingly, he was not carrying a bag or backpack of any kind which would have held his personal belongings.

Surprisingly, and without hesitation she pulled over, stopped her car directly in front of the Traveler and lowered the passenger-side window. Picking up a stranger on the road would never have been something Chelsea would have ever done at any time in her life. It just wasn't something you would do, especially being a woman, but nonetheless, felt compelled to do it.

The Traveler leaned down, allowing each to see one another face to face. The first thing she noticed was that he had soft, kind eyes, which somehow caught her off guard. Not that she had any preconceived notion of what they would look like, or should look like, but they were captivating to say the least, and caused her to hesitate in engaging any conversation with him, making it necessary for Traveler to make the first move.

"Thank you for stopping."

Having had Traveler's words snap her back into consciousness, she immediately responded, "Where you headed?"

"North."

Chelsea was a bit surprised at the ambiguity of his answer.

"Yes, I read your sign. But, just north?"

Traveler saw no need to elaborate. "Just north. Nowhere in particular."

"Everyone has a destination."

Traveler smiled, somewhat baffling Chelsea as to what he could be thinking, or about to say. And his next question confirmed her curious anticipation.

"What would you do if I said, Hell?"
"My first reaction would be, you're too late. You're already there."
"And your second reaction?"

"That it hopefully can be averted, and that maybe I can help you escape the fire."

"Let me guess. You think you can save my soul."

"Does it need saving?"

"That is a debate I look forward to having. Until then, I'll reserve my opinion until I hear what you have to say, if you'll allow me."

"Fair enough. Get in."

Traveler put his walking stick into the back seat and then sat in the front passenger seat, next to Chelsea. Once settled, they drove off.

"You're a brave and trusting woman to dare verbalizing that you could save my soul. The *powers-that-be* wouldn't take kindly to having anyone publicly say that we're living in Hell, or any reference to salvation or Heaven."

"I've survived long enough, and have enough faith at this point that I really don't care what happens. What could they do to me? Kill me?"

Traveler didn't see any need to further the discussion on Chelsea's firm stance. So, he decided on harmless conversation, which did not last long either.

"You asked me where I was headed, but you neglected to tell me where you are headed."

"The opposite of where you're headed, if you think Hell is your final destination, that is."

"So says you."

Chelsea didn't have many opportunities to try and *save* someone's soul, but she was ready to give it her all. "So says God."

"Where is God, these days? I haven't seen much to convince me he's around."

"I take it from your flippant attitude, that you're not a Believer."

"Oh, on the contrary, I firmly believe in the existence of God."

"Your words aren't very convincing... So, is your choice of clothes and carrying a staff supposed to convince me?"

Traveler took the opportunity to flex his muscles in dispute, reciting from the Book of Psalms.

"Yea, though I walk through the valley of the shadow of death, I will fear no EVIL, for thou art with me; thy rod and thy staff they comfort me."

"Well, at least you have the basics down. But Psalm 23 is probably the most quoted of all."

"It's my favorite because I definitely 'fear no EVIL.'"

"Notice that it says, 'thy' rod and staff, not *your* rod and staff."

"If I believe that *my* staff is *thy* staff, and that *thy* staff is *his* staff, then I'm satisfied. Remember, the staff, according to the Scriptures can also be a representation of long suffering."

"Have you been long suffering?"

As if responding under his breath, his answer was not meant to be very audible, but more of an answer to himself, rather than Chelsea.

"If you only knew."

"Really... "

It was more of a concluding statement of uncertainty, than a question. Her curiosity about Traveler allowed her to push further.

"So, you were a man of wealth who lost it all in the pandemic and takeover by the NEW WORLD ORDER, and now, simply a wandering... traveler?"

"Never a man of wealth. But a traveler...for eons."

"Bitter how everything turned out?"

"Not in the least. But I can say with utmost confidence that God had it in for me."

"We're supposed to serve God, not question God."

"Hmm, you're almost starting to sound like God."

"If I do it is because I live to serve Him, so if I sound like him, it is because of that and nothing else."

"Fair enough."

Thinking she would have the last word on the subject, Chelsea injected, "So, you agree that we are not on Earth to question God?"

"To each his own, but for me that's never going to happen."

"Sounds like you need to do more groveling and less complaining if you're ever going to get God's attention to make things better."

"Groveling, begging, pleading, or anything close to it, isn't part of my playbook."

"Mine neither. But for God, if I were you, I'd make the exception."

Traveler smiled, but didn't respond.

"Look, if you want, you can take a nap."

"No, I'm fine. How about you? You feeling okay?"

"Oddly, I'm not tired in the least, and I've been driving now for, hmmm... going on 5 hours straight. I haven't even had a cup of coffee or anything to eat, and I feel fine."

As they continued on their quest, north, Chelsea was stealing looks at her traveling companion, and trying to do so without being caught. Had he noticed, it would have been a great source of embarrassment, especially if he were to think that the perusals were of a flirting nature. Nonetheless, she found him mesmerizing. His long, brown hair was to his shoulders, and left to be free falling. His beard was full and natural, but it was obvious that he had made it a point to keep it well-groomed. What was of most interest to her was that he was dressed in a woolen tunic, tied in the middle with what appeared to be a simple piece of rope. She also observed that he was wearing leather sandals, which were a rarity. She surmised he was either a modern-day caricature of Jesus Christ, or simply a lazed throw-back to the 1960s hippie era, something of which she had only seen in books, when books were allowed.

"You know, we've been on the road now for almost three hours since the last charging station, and, it says I still have a full charge. That just can't be. As a matter of fact, I don't even remember passing any charging stations."

"Maybe God gave you a full charge and you didn't know it. Enjoy it while you can."

"You know, now that I think about it, there have been a lot of things on this trip that don't make sense."

"Like what?"

"Oh, forget about it. Maybe I'm just losing my mind. As a matter of fact, I must be, because I was about to ask you something, but now I forgot what it was."

"You were about to ask if I had a name."

"You actually know what I was *about* to ask you?"

"From experience, I know that it was going to be your next question. I'm pretty good at reading minds."

"That's a scary thought."

"You'll get used to it."

"But, to get back to the question at hand, what *is* your name?"

"My friends just call me Luc."

"How interesting that *ye of little faith* should have such a biblical name. It doesn't get any better than being named Luke."

"It's not Luke, L-U-K-E. It's Luc, L-U-C."

"L-U-C? That's a new one on me. Is it short for something, or is it just L-U-C?"

"It's actually short for Lucifer."

"Oh, come on. Is that a joke? No one would ever name their son, Lucifer. That would be like the worst name ever to give a kid."

"*My* father did. I've really never liked it much, but I swear, it's my God-given name."

"And here I thought that there was only one Lucifer, and now I'm finding out that there's another one. So, your mother and father actually named you Lucifer?"

"Father, but not mother. I really never knew my mother."

Chelsea quickly evolved into a more charitable tone. "I'm sorry. Did she die when you were young?"

"I don't know anything about her. I don't even know if I ever had a mother."

"You had to have had a mother. Unless you were told you simply appeared, and we know that didn't happen."

Traveler smiled to himself, thinking, *If she only knew*----------------- Then again, it was something that he had never considered before.

"Didn't your father ever talk about her, or show you pictures? Something? Anything?"

"Nope. The subject never came up."

"I've gotta be honest with you. I can't call you Luc, Lucifer, or any variation. It just goes against everything I stand for."

"I understand. So, what would you like to call me?"

Chelsea mulled-over the possibilities of what she would call her new-found friend, before coming to a decision. "Maybe I'll just call you *Traveler*."

Traveler smiled, more to himself than to let Chelsea see him, and quietly said, "Afoot and light-hearted I take to the open road, healthy, free, the world before me, the long brown path before me leading wherever I choose."

"Did you just make that up?"

"No. It's from *Song of the Open Road*, by Walt Whitman. It sort of just popped into my head when you decided to call me Traveler."

"Are you okay with it? I thought it kind of filled in all of the gaps of who you are, what you are, and what you are doing."

"I definitely like it."

"Then, *Traveler* it is. Are you interested in knowing my name?

"I already know your name. It's Chelsea."

Chelsea was in shock, but it somehow didn't really affect her general demeanor. Under normal circumstances it would have scared her that a complete stranger knew her name.

"I'd ask how you knew that, but you already told me you can read minds. Do you have any other...gifts, that I should be aware of, or concerned with?"

"I am proudly a person of many talents - Teacher, philosopher, ...and prankster.

"Prankster? That's one I've never heard anyone describe himself as."

"It's my favorite."

"Do I dare ask you to elaborate?"

"It'll become evident soon enough."

"I'll take your word for it. You know, I'm also a teacher."

"Let me guess. High school history."

"Exactly! Okay, there are a million possibilities of what kind of teacher I am, so what made you guess that I was a history teacher?"

"I didn't guess. I can read minds. Remember?"

"Now, you're scaring me."

"Actually, you're not scared at all. Intrigued, maybe a little curious, but definitely not scared."

Traveler was right. Chelsea wasn't scared in the least, though everything about their chance meeting and his ability to read her mind, or so he said, would have raised the hairs on the back of her neck in fear of this stranger, and yet, it wasn't the case. Though Traveler already knew the answers to any questions he was asking, he tried to make the conversation as normal as possible, until such time as she would come to accept him and his abilities.

"You haven't said, but I assume you're headed home?"

"Yes. Well, home, meaning where I was born and raised."

"Do you make this drive often?"

"Pre-pandemic, usually twice a year. Sometimes, three times, if I got there for Thanksgiving. But now it has been almost four years.

"That's a long time."

"Things changed after my mother and father died in the pandemic of '29. Before that, it was another four years. The pandemic sure made visiting family a very difficult thing to do. Now, I'm going to visit my two brothers. They're all I have left."

"I take it you're not teaching anymore."

"Teaching what? How to worship EVIL? Besides, public schools aren't really schools anymore. They're simply indoctrination centers and I'm not interested."

"Careful. That kind of talk can get you in a lot of trouble."

"Not any more than I've already been in."

"You honestly don't strike me as the *getting into trouble'* type."

"I didn't used to be. But it got to the point where I just couldn't take it anymore. I figured that the worst that could happen was they would euthanize me, which would mean that the worst thing that could ever happen on Earth would be the best thing to finally get me to where I have been heading for, my entire life."

"Which is?"

"Heaven."

"You'd be willing to die for a cause just to get to Heaven?"

"For the right cause, yes. And fighting the NEW WORLD ORDER, which is just a cover-up for it's true name, EVIL, is just such a cause."

"Have you been fighting them?"

"The best I could. I went underground with a bunch of same-thinking people, until…well…we were arrested and sent to Pendleton for re-programming."

"You hesitated. You don't remember when you were sent to Pendleton?"

"I think it was just a couple of days ago. But I don't know how that would be possible. You know, somehow, it's all a blur."

"And yet, here you are, seemingly quite aware of everything."

"Oh God, I hope I'm not going insane."

"I wouldn't worry about that. As a matter of fact, I am positive you haven't lost your mind."

"As they say, from your lips to God's ears, I sure hope that I'm not."

Traveler smiled at the interjection of *God* into the conversation.

"Do you think that you can win the war against EVIL; meaning of course, the NEW WORLD ORDER?"

"On my own, No. I need God's help, but in spite of endless prayers he seems to be sitting on the sidelines, much to my...."

Chelsea didn't finish the sentence.

"Anger?"

"You said it. I didn't."

"But you were definitely thinking it."

"Oh, I forgot, you can read minds."

"You think that God let you down?"

"In a way. At the very least he should have begun the Rapture. At least we would have had something to look forward to."

"You sound pretty bitter."

"I don't mean to be, or want to be, but by God not giving us his Wrath to fight EVIL, or the Rapture to end EVIL's reign and finally reward the GOOD, is like a millionaire outliving his kids and never having given them even ten cents of their inheritance. What's the point in having all that power?"

"I'm sure that one of these days you will get the opportunity to ask him."

"And when that day comes, the first thing I'm going to say to God is, "Where Was Your Wrath When We Needed It?""

"I'd like to be there to hear his answer."

"Well, just keep in mind that to hear me ask it, and hear him answer it, that you'll have to be dead also."

"I can see that we're off the main highway. We must be getting close to your home."

"Something tells me that you don't need me to confirm what you seem to already know."

Chelsea came to a stop sign on the two-lane country road, looked both ways, and turned right.

Traveler, almost as if talking to himself, but with the full attention of his traveling companion, continued. "I shall be telling this with a sigh. Somewhere ages and ages hence: Two roads diverged in a wood, and I— I took the one less traveled by, and that has made all the difference."

Chelsea was intrigued with the quote, of origin unknown, but felt compelled to ask.

"That is quite beautiful. But I'm not familiar with it, except that I know it's not biblical."

"You're right. It's from a poem by Robert Frost, titled *The Road Not Taken*."

"Oh, Frost. Of course. I've heard the name, but I'm not familiar with his writings."

"And you, a history teacher, aren't familiar with him? He was a gifted poet, who actually won four Pulitzer Prizes in his lifetime, in and of the times when winning a Pulitzer actually meant something. By most standards, he was a genius."

"Nope. Not really."

"Where have you been?"

"For the past eight years I'm afraid that my studies of literature were restricted to trying to find my way around the NEW WORLD ORDER through the Scriptures. I never had time to read anything else."

"And before that?"

"My mother said that our education wasn't what it used to be or should have been. Maybe that's what she was talking about."

"I take it you were close to your mother."

"Very. I miss her so much. You would have loved her. Everybody did. She would have treated you like one of her own. It's was one of her most redeeming qualities. She loved everyone, and made everyone feel loved. That and the fact that she thought that every meal was a banquet."

"She sounds like she was a good woman."

"The best."

"We don't know each other very well, but let me leave this thought with you. There's so much more to life, and to learn, than what's in the Bible."

"Not for me. All of life's questions are answered in the Bible."

"You can't take ten questions and think that one verse will answer all of them."

"I disagree."

"Is that why you ignore the teachings, and lessons, of others who aren't in the Bible. How can you be so sure that, say, a man like Robert Frost wasn't an emissary of God? Maybe he had just as much to offer as say, Matthew, Mark, John, Luke, or any other of the biblical prophets."

Chelsea thought about what Traveler had just said.

"Okay, fine. Strictly for the sake of research, was there an intended lesson in Frost's writings?"

"Thank you for opening up your mind. The short answer is, most definitely. At least I found it to be so. Basically, he was telling us to not travel the same route as everyone else, but, if and when you do, you will undoubtedly have a different result. But the lesson is that no matter what happens, you should not only be satisfied with the outcome, but without regret to have had it come out any other way."

Chelsea thought about it for a few moments, before challengingly responding. *"Enter through the narrow gate. For wide is the gate and broad is the road that leads to destruction, and many enter through it. But small is the gate and narrow the road that leads to life, and only a few find it"*

Traveler was impressed with Chelsea's knowledge of Scripture, yet determined for her to open her mind to everything else that is out there.

" Somewhat shallow thinking. Matthew says there is only a small gate and a narrow road. But Frost offers more hope than Matthew, as it doesn't matter which path, or road, you choose. For Frost, with either path you win, and no one, not even you, should ever question the choice. Matthew, however, is clear, that although there are two choices, one leads to destruction, and one to salvation. How are you to know which one to choose?"

"If there's any doubt, then you must have chosen the wrong path many times before. If you want further proof, look to Jeremiah 6:16. Thus says the Lord, 'Stand by the roads, and look, and ask for the ancient paths, where the good way is; and walk in it, and find rest for your souls.'"

Traveler was enjoying the debate, yet, was fearful that she would see his challenging stance as being critical, and not playfully challenging. Not ceding to her position, Traveler ended the conversation on this note-

"'But they said, we will not walk in it.' Obviously, man will always be conflicted as to which road, or which person, to follow. Man has to be led by the hand and shown the way. He is not capable of always choosing correctly for himself."

While Chelsea was contemplating what to say as a retort, Traveler calmly allowed Chelsea to absorb all that he had said. As they continued down the two-lane country road, in the heart of Sonoma, Traveler was observing the miles and miles of vineyards on either side of the road. Traveler still allowed Chelsea to fill in the blanks, even though Traveler was well aware of the answers before posing the questions.

"From the landscape, I take it that your family is in the winery business?"

"Four generations."

"But, obviously not you. Was teaching a life-long ambition?"

"For me, it was anything but farming. I wanted nothing to do with it. Too many headaches. Not enough water, too much water, not enough sun, too much sun, bugs, disease, fires. Fires are the worst."

"Yeah, I'm sure that whole idea of *fire* can be pretty daunting."

"Not that I have any first-hand knowledge, but fires in a grape-field are probably just as nasty as the Fires of Hell.

"Maybe so, though the fires in a grape field eventually go out."

"You wouldn't think that, if you've ever seen how long it takes to clear the ash, replant, and regrow a field of grapes. It can take years."

"So, you just...left?"

"Yup. When I graduated from high school and made up my mind that I was going to be a teacher, I told both of my brothers, it's all yours. And I walked away with no regrets."

When they got to the front entrance to the driveway, the gate was chained shut. The sign on the gate read, "No trespassing. By order of the NEW WORLD ORDER."

"What? This doesn't make any sense. I just talked to my brothers two weeks ago. They said everything was fine. That it looked like it was going to be the best crop in ten years."

After getting out of the car, Chelsea reached down and pulled the sign up to get a better look. Suddenly they noticed an old woman walking down the side of the road, coming toward them. When she finally reached them, she stopped.

"If you're looking for the Smith boys, you're too late. They're gone."
"Where'd they go?"
"Not really sure. One of those NEW WORLD ORDER prison vans drove up a few days ago, arrested the two boys and off they went."
"To where?"
"To where do you think? When you are arrested by those devils, you are never coming back."

Chelsea fell back against the car and dropped her head, in shock and disbelief at what she had just heard. In the blink of an eye, the NEW WORLD ORDER has erased her family from existence. And for what? The only answer that seemed to be the common one, in cases like was, "Because they could."

"No reason?"

"They don't give a reason. Oh, they filled the local videos at the charging stations for two days with a warning that the *Farm* was punishment for anyone with a family member who is a dissident to the NEW WORLD ORDER."

Chelsea tried to wipe the tears from her face.

"You the sister?"
"Yes, how'd you know."
"Been expecting you."
"Why?"
"Not that it will make things any better, but when they took your brothers away, one of them kept yelling, 'Tell my sister she did the right thing.' ...And now I've told you."
"Thank you."
"You're welcome... I'm just curious. What exactly did you do?"
"I refused to obey."

In a faint voice in which her parting words were barely able to be heard, Chelsea heard here say, "Yeah, that's what I did also...Heaven help us."

Traveler immediately became the consoling presence in the shocking emptiness that Chelsea was now experiencing.

"This has to be quite a shock. I'm sorry."
"What? Sorry that I got my brothers killed?"
"You didn't get them killed. The NEW WORLD ORDER got them killed."
"What difference does it make anymore? It's not like there is anything I can do about it. I'm an orphan. No family, no job. No money. No plans. I'm lost."

Traveler didn't hesitate to fill the void with the words from another famous poem of centuries past.

"...I once was lost, but now I am found,
Was blind, but now I see.
'Twas grace that taught my heart to fear,
And grace my fears relieved.'"

"Another one of your poets? It's beautiful, but I'm afraid that words cannot replace my brothers."

"No, but sometimes they can ease the memories and repair the loss."

"I don't know how."

"Then you should hear the rest before you decide."

Traveler continued-----

"How precious did that grace appear
The hour I first believed.
Through many dangers, toils and snares
I have already come,
'Tis grace has brought me safe thus far
And grace will lead me home.
The Lord has promised good to me
His word my hope secures;
He will my shield and portion be,
As long as life endures.
Yea, when this flesh and heart shall fail,
And mortal life shall cease
I shall possess within the veil,
A life of joy and peace.

When we've been there ten thousand years
Bright shining as the sun,
We've no less days to sing God's praise
Than when we've first begun.'

The author's name is John Newton. He wrote that in 1779."

"I have to admit. It's beautiful."

"Just trying to reinforce what I said before. Life isn't just about Scripture. It's a beautiful world, and there is much to be learned by the words of mortal man, even a non-Prophet and clergyman, like John Newton."

"Newton was a clergyman?"

"Yes. Did that make him a better writer? I think not."

"Getting to know you has certainly been an education."

"And it's about to get even more so, very soon."

"I don't understand what you're getting at."

"Chelsea. It's time to move on."

"And go where?"

"To the Road not taken, thus far."

"Again, I don't understand."

"Just follow me. It'll all become very clear to you in the next few minutes."

Traveler opened the gate and pulled it aside for Chelsea to enter.

"I thought it had a lock on it."

"It did, but we're way beyond locks, now."

His choice of words had Chelsea concerned. As they came upon the graves of her parents, they stopped.

"As odd as it may seem, I'm sort of thankful that my parents didn't live to see this world we live in, and my brothers killed the way they were. I wish I had some flowers. My mother always loved fresh flowers. Her favorite were peonies."

And with a wave of his hand, Traveler filled the earth above the graves of her parents with an abundance of fresh flowers of multiple varieties, including the most beautiful peonies she had ever seen. Chelsea looked over at the Traveler, almost in disbelief that he could do that, but immediately accepted that it could only be possible if Traveler wasn't who she thought him to be. Obviously, he wasn't some ordinary hitchhiker, now in her life without purpose.

"What you just did was nothing short of a miracle. How did you do that?"

"God gave me the power."

"Are you...an angel?"

"Archangel, to be more specific."

"You're an Archangel? But why are you here? With me?"

"Why do you think?"

"I don't know. This is all very confusing. Are you here to help me do something?"

"Maybe, many things. God hasn't been very clear just yet on what he has in store for you."

"God? God sent you to be with me?"

"Yes."

There was a long hesitation before Chelsea asked the next question, almost fearful of what the answer would be.

"Am I dead?"

"Yes."

Traveler had always found that most were not surprised to hear that they were dead. Some were surprised to hear how they died, and others angry at being sent to Hell, but most dealt with their deaths in a calm manner.

"For how long?"

"Seconds, minutes, one day, meaning today. Time really isn't a measure of anything, once you're dead."

"Now it makes sense. On our trip I wasn't tired. I wasn't hungry. And when we were in the charging station, the policemen didn't even scan me."

"Because they didn't see you. You weren't actually there, to them."

"But I don't remember dying. I wasn't even sick."

"But you remember being arrested and brought to Pendleton."

"Yes. Of course. When I was arrested, I was told that it was necessary to be reeducated, which really meant that they were going to try and program me to be one of their NEW WORLD ORDER stooges."

"Reeducating you was never their intention. They knew they could never change your mind about anything."

"You mean, that when they escorted all of us into the classroom, it wasn't really a classroom?"

"No. It was a gas chamber. Within two minutes, you and the other hundred with you, were dead."

"Not that it matters now, but what did they do with us?"

"Brought you out to the crematorium and turned you to ash. I'm not here to sugarcoat your demise, but that's exactly what happened."

"The same for my brothers?"

"Yes."

Chelsea was heartbroken at hearing the final confirmation that her brothers were also "eliminated."

"So, going to the Farm was just another way of saying that they were going to a death camp?"

"Exactly. Not that it will make this any easier for you, but they went down fighting. They were good men."

"I suppose if I were alive, I'd be crying right now. But somehow, I can't."

"No, you can't. The dead can't cry. Well, at least the GOOD can't. On the other hand, those who have gone to Hell, cry a lot."

"Okay, I'm fine with the *being dead* thing. But if you're an Archangel, then which one are you? Michael? Gabriel? Raphaël?

"Keep going… You're getting hotter… no pun intended. You have one more guess."

"Four more."

"I'm here to help and guide you, not to debate how many Archangels there are."

"But I already know there are seven."

"Actually, the correct answer is Four."

"Seven."

"Seven, if you believe what Enoch surmised in his own mind. He had no proof, until he died, and then he found out that there were only two."

"You just said there were four."

"Two that were left in Heaven when Enoch got there."

"Why are you doing this?"

"Doing what?"

"Trying to confuse me."

"I'm not trying to confuse you. I'm just trying to educate you. Originally, there were three sons of God. And the three sons were the original Archangels. And then when Junior came along, that made four."

"Who is Junior?"

"Who is Junior? Are you serious? Jesus. The Son of God. The reason for the New Testament. Number Four. And in case you're wondering, which I know you are, it goes like this - Michael is Number 1. Lucifer is Number Two. Gabriel is Number Three. And Jesus is Number Four. Now do you get the picture?"

"Mmm, not really."

"Okay, let me pose it to you this way. If I'm not Michael, and I'm not Gabriel, and I'm not Jesus, but I am one of the sons of God, and an Archangel to boot, then who am I?"

Chelsea's eyes widened at the revelation of whom she was talking to.

"Nooo, Way."

"Yesss, Way."

"You're Lucifer? *The* Lucifer? Not just some traveler name Lucifer?"

"As I live and breathe...sort of."

"Ahh, what do you take me for? Do I honestly come across as that gullible?"

"So, if I were an angel or Archangel by any other name you'd be fine with it, but because I am Lucifer, *The* Lucifer, sometimes also known as the Devil, Satan, Beelzebub, all of a sudden you're *not* fine with it.?"

"But..."

"Oh, I see. No horns, no talons for fingers, no pointed tail, and no bright red complexion from spending too much time near the fires of Hell, so how could I possibly be the real Lucifer?"

"Exactly."

"You know, sometimes Homo Sapiens astound me with how much of Sapien is a misnomer."

"You're really Lucifer? The Prince of Hell?"

"The one and only. You got a problem with that?"

"Of course I have a problem with that. Wait- Oh my God. Am I in Hell?"

"No. Not even close."

"Then why are *you* here?"

"It's complicated. As part of my penance, God has arranged for me to take you under wing, metaphorically speaking, and guide you through this phase of your death."

Chelsea immediately brought-up *in her mind* that the Bible clearly warns that Satan and his demons may take on human form, and cautions that in his attempts to deceive us, he may even seem like a messenger from God. "Satan himself masquerades as an angel of light" (2 Corinthians 11:14). It is a warning that even Lucifer, in human form, could have a mesmerizing or intoxicating effect, conjuring an aura of trust."

"I heard that! So, let me try and make this as easy on you as possible. I'm not masquerading as anything or anybody except as myself. I'm not here to deceive you, or tempt you in any way. I'm here, with you, as a favor to God."

"Favor? He didn't just command you?"

"Favor, command... In his own way, they're one in the same."

"I am so confused right now. If you're Lucifer, but this isn't Hell, then what is it?"

Traveler was beginning to realize that this task wasn't going to be as easy as he had figured on, and vented his frustration aloud. "No wonder Gabe and Mikey passed on this."

"Passed on what?"

"On breaking the news to you that you're dead, and having to deal with this."

"Again, I'm not sure what that means. And who exactly are Gabe and Mikey?"

"Gabriel and Michael. I've been on Earth for so long that I now refer to them as having earthly nicknames."

"Why would God send the Devil to help me if I'm not in Hell?"

"Again, it's complicated. Yes, I am Lucifer. Yes, I am the Devil, as humans refer to me, but it really isn't accurate. For now, just accept that I'm here to help you make the final journey to Heaven."

"So, if this isn't Hell, and it isn't Heaven, where are we?"

"You're in a way station."

"What's a way station? Is it like Purgatory?"

"I'm not at liberty to divulge why you're here, exactly. Generally, when a person with your resume is on her way to Heaven, you just go. But God said to hold you here."

"For what? Why?"

"I didn't ask, and he didn't say."

"Does this happen very often?"

"Every couple hundred years or so."

"So it *is* Purgatory?"

"What do you know about Purgatory? You're not even Catholic."

"My mom was Catholic, and she talked about it all the time. I never actually knew my Uncle Joey, but my Mom said that he was such a screw-up, that when he died he probably was doomed to life-everlasting in Purgatory."

"Ohhh, Joey. I remember your Uncle Joey. Boy, when he found out there was no beer in Purgatory, he became a handful."

"You knew my Uncle Joey?"

"Of course, Joey and I got to know one another pretty well."

"Was Purgatory like going to AA for him?"

"Not just AA, but he had a problem with gambling, and a few other addictions that I can't talk about. To be up front, he was a real borderline case, meaning if Purgatory wasn't around, he would have definitely gone straight to Hell."

"So, Purgatory is a real thing?"

"For Catholics it is. God tries to accommodate all belief systems so he made sure there is a Purgatory."

"How about for non-Catholics?"

"God doesn't discriminate. Call it what you want, but most are deserving of a second chance, so Purgatory, by any name, if necessary, is where you go to clean up a bit before the final ascent."

"That's really good to know."

"If it'll make things any better, your uncle cleaned up his act and finally made it out."

"That's great news. My mother would be so happy."

"She already knows. I also met your parents, while on their way. You were right. Very nice people."

"Oh yeah, that makes sense. So, getting back to my original question - If you're really Lucifer, and we're not in Hell, then why are *you* here?"

"Again, it's complicated. As I said, you are a part of my penance."

"Now, I'm really confused. How can I be part of *your* penance? Are you in Purgatory also?"

"More or less. I've done a few million bad things in the past, and part of my penance is to do favors for God, from time to time."

"You must be really special to have done a few million bad things and not have gone straight to Hell."

"Well, I *am* a son of God. And I actually did go straight to Hell, but I'm not restricted to Hell, like mortals. I'm sort of an enigma. Being a son of God does have its perks, in spite of being who I am."

"You don't live in Hell?"

"Nope. Never have. I go back and forth to welcome the EVIL and the DAMNED, but actually, I live on Earth, with Man, and have since the Garden of Eden."

"Wow. So, tell me. What's God like?"

"Exactly like everything you've ever imagined. But it's that way for everybody. When they meet God, he looks exactly like the person imagined. God is really good at doing that."

"Oh, I'm so happy to hear that."

"So, I'm not going to Hell?"

"No."

"What do I have to do to take the next step to Heaven?"

"God hasn't shared that part yet. But I can assure you that I'm here on direct orders from God. He didn't send a dove, brother Gabriel, or any other imagination of Man. He told me himself."

"That is so awesome. You mean, like, he showed up in person? In the flesh?"

"To you, he would have shown up looking human, just as you would have imagined him. But to me, no."

"I see. How does he show up to you?"

"In ways you'd never understand."

"I'm good with that. So, seeing as you're here with me, any clues as to why?"

"From past experience, it probably has something to do with you not accepting your death."

"How could anyone know I haven't accepted my death? I just found out five minutes ago that I was even dead."

"Okay, you have to accept that this is God we're talking about."

"Ohhh...I get it. God knew I wouldn't accept my death because he knew I wouldn't accept my death before I even died."

"What do you say we start this process with baby steps? You need to listen to me and listen closely. This is not Purgatory. It's simply a way station. God clearly has a reason for you to be here, and for me to be here with you. So, let's just calm down and let the process play out. Okay?"

"God, you don't have to get angry. If that's the way it's got to be, then…fine."

"Thank you. Now, follow me."

They walked down the cobble-stone path around the side of the house, a path that had been put-in almost seventy years ago by Chelsea's great-grandfather. When they reached the back of the house, Chelsea stopped to see what had once been hundreds of acres of grapevines and was now a garden paradise. There were flowers of ever variety imaginable, and trees disbursed amongst the flowers.

"What's this? Our property never looked like this. Where are all of the grapevines? It would be hard to imagine that even the Garden of Eden looked this good."

"This *is* the Garden of Eden."

"Are you serious? The actual Garden of Eden?"

"Just like it's been for…. well, since the Beginning."

"It's beautiful."

"It's supposed to be."

"You know, I've always been curious about something. If God had decided to do it, what would have been the first animal that he would have put here?"

"If you have to ask, then obviously you don't know as much about the Book of Genesis as you pretend."

"What are you talking about?"

"There *were* animals here. As soon as Eve took a bite from the apple, the birds and the bees showed up."

Chelsea thought about it for a second before responding.

"That's supposed to be a joke, right? Adam and Eve became ashamed which meant they lost their innocence and were now aware of their nakedness."

"Adam and Eve, sitting in a tree…and then the birds and the bees helped them create Cain, Abel, and Seth."

"Something tells me that you don't take anything seriously. Everything with you is fun and games."

"Fun and games is the foundation of being a prankster."

"I somehow get the feeling that there isn't enough penance in the world to get you back in the good graces of God."

"I have it on good authority that you are my final test."

"Then, for starters, I really need to know why I'm here. And especially why I'm here with you."

"Eventually, all that God has planned for you will reveal itself. But for now, just try and accept that I am here to be your mentor, your conscience, and your guide."

"Why did God choose you to be here, now, with me? And why does God think that the Devil would make a good mentor?"

"Just go along with the program. Please? You just need to give the Devil his due…"

"Yeah, yeah, yeah…You know it's jokes like that."

"Actually, it was a pun."

"Whatever. But I'm still not convinced of everything you've been telling me. For starters, if I seem to be under some misinformation about certain things, especially who and what you are, then tell me why God threw you out of Heaven."

"I've sort of always been a renegade, meaning that I'm obviously not one to simply do as you're told."

"Even from God?"

"Especially from God. Who does he think he is?"

Chelsea looked at him, very confused, before responding.

"Oh, that was another joke. You know, I've only known you for a few hours and I'm already siding with God."

"Well, the long and short it is that he told me to get out. And when I said No, in the snap of his fingers, using symbolism you understand, he invented Hell, and gave me the boot."

"How long has it been?"

"Time, for us, really isn't something that is understandable for Man. Let's just say, *pre*, Garden of Eden."

"And you still haven't apologized?"

"Hell, no. If I went back, I'd just be sitting around like my brothers, for eons on end, doing nothing. You know, I really like Earth, and the people of Earth. It's going to be hard for me, when it's over."

"You mean after the Rapture?"

"For me, it'll simply be the End of Times. I'm going to miss it. All of it."

"Maybe God will try again. Maybe even fix a few of the mistakes."

"No, I wouldn't like that. I've come to know and love the flaws and failures of Man. There was never a dull moment. I've had a lot of fun over the millennia watching Man make a fool out of himself at every turn. Man hasn't gotten much right, ever, and of late it has been very costly. I think you can personally attest to that."

"Okay, wait a minute. How are you going to miss it? You're an Archangel. You don't have feelings."

"Feelings, no. But there is definitely a deep sense of sympatico with Man."

"Even EVIL Man?"

"No. Even I, Lucifer, had to draw the line there. The ever-presence of EVIL over the centuries has made my life a living Hell, with everyone believing that somehow, I am responsible for their actions."

"You expect me to believe that you're *not*?"

"Most definitely, *not*. One thing Man has never been good at is accepting responsibility for his transgressions. It's always someone else's fault. So, Man has aways needed a scapegoat, and you're looking at him."

"So, You're trying to tell me that you're the most misunderstood person ever."

"No, that honor goes to God. What I *am*, is the biggest scapegoat in the history of the Universe, for all of the EVILs in the world that have befallen Man. But it's okay. I'm pretty thick-skinned."

"You're Lucifer. How can you possibly claim to be a scapegoat, for anything whatsoever?"

"Because my very existence is totally misunderstood. I already alluded to it."

"It sounds to me like you have a lot of explaining to do. Maybe we should go back to the beginning and give me the Lucifer version of everything that has happened since the beginning of time, meaning since you were cast out from Heaven."

Lucifer thought about it for a while and said, "All of it?"

"From the beginning, up to and including right now. Remember, the Devil is in the details."

Traveler was amused by her play on words, thinking it something to be proud of.

"You see, I can take it, and give it."

"Well, just for the record, I fell off my dinosaur the first time I heard that one."

"I've really never been, *EVIL*. Mischievous, most definitely. But, EVIL? Never. I get my kicks out of tempting the supposed *GOOD* with anything and everything to get them to cross over to the dark side, for even a second. It's pretty funny to watch it happen, and to see the reaction of their friends and family, and eventually themselves. But beyond that, Man has always been on his own to make his own choices."

"And God lets you do it?"

"Yes, because of the bet."

"What bet?"

"*The* bet. The first bet. Where I bet with my Father that given the chance, meaning if I tempted them with a chance at gaining *knowledge* of themselves and their surroundings, that they would do it. I actually invented the Tree of Knowledge to prove my point"

"Of course you did. But God already knew what they would do."

"He did, but as they say, seeing is believing. So, when I proposed the bet, he said that he would allow Adam and Eve to decide for themselves. What it proved, and what it did, was for God to never stop Man from being Man, and doing what Man will choose to do, whether it be GOOD or EVIL. It's why God invented penitence. There's always a way back, but Man has to make the decision on his own."

"Is there any chance that you'll do the same?"

"The same what?

"That you'll recognize your evil ways, repent, and fight for GOOD?"

"Okay. If I'm going to help you, you're going to have to have a change in attitude. For starters, that means accepting that I, the

Archangel Lucifer, don't have any *evil* ways. Though, I have to admit, that because of thousands of years of misinformation, that you, with the help of some…writers in the Bible that you hold so dear, mistakenly see me as the *symbol* of EVIL. I have really never committed an EVIL act in my entire life- excuse me, existence. Not a crime to be found, unless you consider a little bit of aiding and abetting. Not even *you* can find a place in the Bible where I actually committed an EVIL act."

Chelsea immediately began scanning the Bible in her mind, trying to think of an EVIL act.

"What about, by your own admission, tempting Eve in the Garden of Eden?"

"Hellooo…*tempting* is not *forcing*. And another thing. I hate snakes, so I would have never appeared to anyone as a snake, serpent or anything other than another living, human being…You know, before this is over, I hope that you will have a better grasp of symbolism, especially as it relates to the Bible."

"So, when are you going to give it up and do the right thing?"

"I can see that with the obvious end of Man, as I have come to know him, it looks like sooner rather than later. When Man ceases to exist, I have already accepted that I'm going to have to put my tail between my legs, metaphorically, apologize, and give up my earthly ways."

"You sound like you're going to regret having to apologize."

"It's not like I haven't known, *that day* would come. Truthfully, I think that being down here annoys my brothers more than my Father. They're such… brown nosers and goody two-sandals".

"I think the expression is goody two-*shoes*."

"They've never worn shoes. And only Jesus ever wore sandals."

"Hellooo. And you."

Traveler had to recognize that he was wearing sandals.

" Okay. So, you got me on that one…Goody two-bare-feet would be more accurate than two-*shoes,* though the only time that becomes apparent is when we are meeting arrivals for the first time, in human form, in Heaven. When you get to Heaven, you'll see what I mean."

"What was it like in the beginning? Before the Garden of Eden?

"All there was, was Heaven."

"I know what Genesis says: '*In the beginning God created the heaven and the earth'.*"

"For starters, you need to pay attention more to the words, which, as we will discuss later, is a big problem with Man."

"Enlighten me, then."

"The *beginning*, in Genesis, doesn't refer to *the Heaven.* It refers to the *heaven*, small H, meaning what Man knows as his universe: the sky, the sun, the moon, the stars, the planets, and infinite space. Heaven, capital H, is where God lives. Where my brothers and I lived. Where the GOOD go after death. Understand?"

"Of course I understand. But it's not what I've been taught, so it's hard to accept."

"Give it time. It'll sink in. Now, to continue…Being in Heaven was pretty boring. Think about it. There was God, and Michael, the first-created, then me, and then Gabriel. No games, no pets, no nothing. So, we had to find things to keep us busy, the first of which were sports games, which for the record came long before the Greeks held their first Olympic Games in 776 BC. which were held as a tribute to Zeus."

"But, Zeus wasn't real."

"He was real to them. But God never complained or tried to change their mind, as any worship to a supreme being, or God, no matter how flawed, theoretically was a tribute to God."

"One day, an argument arose between Gabriel and me."

"How come you didn't say, between Gabriel and myself?"

"The best reason I can think of, is that saying, "between Gabriel and *myself*," would be incorrect, and you, being a teacher, should know that. To continue... Gabriel thought that he had thrown a javelin farther than I had. I disagreed."

"Question- How far can a son of God throw a javelin?"

"What's that got to do with anything?"

"A human can only throw it, hmmm...I don't even know how far a man can throw a javelin."

"The farthest on record is a little over one-hundred meters. But we had a way of dialing down our powers to make ability and technique a component to make it easier to record the distance. And for the record, doing so was part of the blueprint that my father utilized in creating Adam. May I continue?"

"Please do."

"An argument developed, and before you knew it, two of God's perfect children were involved in a full-blown Donnybrook, and that was eons before the Irish had even been invented. Not that the concept of winning and losing, anything, had been figured out at that point, but when it looked like Gabriel was going down for the count Michael jumped in to help Gabriel."

"Stop. What does that mean, *going down for the count*? You were Archangels. You couldn't feel pain or anger, or anything else, so what was the point?"

"Good call. We never even considered that…It didn't matter. Before it got any uglier, meaning that Good Old Dad was witnessing something he never expected, and contrary to his plan for his perfect children, he waved his hand and ended it."

"Good for God! But I take it that God wasn't big on the *Boys will be Boys* aspect of this whole thing?"

"Not even close. After a nasty tongue-lashing for allowing it to get to that point, he said he wanted all three of us to apologize to one another, agree to never let it happen again, and to put it behind us as though it had never happened."

"But something tells me, you weren't willing to do that."

"*Hell*, no. Why would I be willing to let bygones be bygones when I was stopped from winning a fight, by a brother who then beat me until I was silly, by human standards. I had every reason to reject the apology-ending order. Remember, never apologize. It's a sign of weakness. So, I told my father, *No*."

Chelsea looked at Traveler in questioning disbelief.

"You told God, *No*?!"

"That's *so* interesting. He had the same reaction. And I'd be willing to bet that since that happened, at a time that is immeasurable by human comprehension, no one has dared to ever do it again. Well, no one in Heaven that is."

"And?"

"Contrary to Man's beliefs, I can assure you that God does *not* have a sense of humor. He *appreciates* a good sense of humor, but really never found it necessary to actually have one, himself."

"And?"

"And, as they say, the rest is history."

"Getting used to you is going to take some real patience."

"Heh, it is what it is."

"And then you were cast into the Lake of Fire, or Hell."

"Again, don't believe everything you read. We're back to symbolism. Look, by human standards, Hell is an ugly place of constant suffering. And a place for man, not for angels. Saying *No* isn't punishable by an eternity of suffering for a son of God.

"But there is a Hell?

"Of course. But it didn't get used as the Hell you know, until Cain killed Abel"

"You know, that actually makes sense... So, what did you do?"

"After Dad cast me out of Heaven, I pretty much wandered the universes, and yes, there are an infinite number of them, with one being as boring as the next, looking for something to do to pass the time."

"I thought that "time" was not a thing for angels."

"It's not, meaning that now you understand how boring it really was. Anyway, I really didn't get my big break until God put Adam and Eve into the Garden. It opened up a whole new world for me."

"You did it again, didn't you?"

"Just making sure you're paying attention. With Adam and Eve now in the Garden, it was easy for me to assume the same image. And that is how I appeared to them. This whole serpent thing was the imagination of Man."

"Wow."

"Wow, is right! I now had a place to go, and things to do... After winning the bet, I was around for the birth of all three of the children."

"Cain, Abel, and Seth."

"At least the scribes of the Old Testament got that part right. The bottom line is that, with a place to go and people to talk to, it was as if the weight of the world had been lifted off of my shoulders, which Atlas certainly would have appreciated."

Chelsea looked at him.

"I couldn't resist… It didn't take long to appreciate that I was out from under Dad's watchful eye, and wrath, as it were, for good. I took-on the image of Man, actually millions of times, and lived out the ages.

"You can never be out from under God's watchful eye."

"You can if he's decided not to talk to you, or have anything to do with you, until such time as I came back to apologize. And to my credit, I never have."

"Oh, you must be *so* proud of yourself."

"I am. Very proud. I've been quite happy for eons, doing whatever I wanted to do and whenever I've wanted to do it.

Chelsea was having a hard time accepting Lucifer, the rogue Archangel.

"So, Hell isn't as nasty as we've been led to believe it is?"

"For Man it is. But the imagery isn't quite accurate. Thanks to the likes of Matt and Luke, the generations have been convinced that Hell is all about fire, crying, wailing, pain and suffering. Oh, and let's not forget the fires and darkness, which when said in the same breath seems kind of silly as you can't really have darkness around the flames from a good ole barn burner. At least not in the earthly sense of the word. Maybe tonight we should have a giant bonfire to give you an idea. Maybe even break out the makings for S'mores. I invented them you know."

"I don't believe that, for even a second."

"It's true. What was the point of all those fires without having something to do with them?"

For Chelsea, she could now see how others, even of a person of strong faith could fall for his deceitfulness. He was charming, playful, and inviting, which was meant to suck you in and make you let your guard down.

"And another thing, now that we're discussing my past life as an Archangel, I've also never been happy that I ended up with the name, Lucifer. And I'm not that fond of *Satan*, either. I should have stopped those early scribes, centuries ago, from calling me that."

"Then, what should I call you, if Lucifer bothers you so much?"

"I was always fond of Asmodeus, the Hebrew name for me, but that name has eviler attachments to it than Lucifer. To make matters worse, when Junior came along, and the Christians decided they needed the New Testament, somehow Lucifer became the go-to name. So, I'm stuck with it."

"Junior? Oh, yeah, Jesus."

"Exactly. I'm still a little baffled by the human infatuation with the last born. Please...Let's move onto another subject."

"Like what?"

"Like, me. Do you know what is the most interesting thing about being me? Every religion has their own God, in one form or another, but those very same religions, be it Christianity, Judaism, Buddhism, Islam, to name a few of the bigger ones, pretty much have the same view of the Devil, Satan, Lucifer, the Prince of Darkness, or whatever it is they wish to call me. Don't you find that interesting? All are on the same page, so to speak about the nature of EVIL, but none of them ever figured out that they needed to have a concentrated unification in order to *defeat* EVIL, and that had better change quickly."

"Why did God create Man?"

"He never really said, but I like to think it had something to do with giving me a purpose."

"You think that creating Man, was all about you?"

"Who else would it be about? If you think about it, when God created Adam and Eve, I was already there, looking for something to do."

"Oh, so he was just being a good father, and providing you with playmates?"

"You know, that just might be it!"

"Okay, but how did God create Man in his own image?"

"God created a bunch of different prototypes of Man, using himself, until he found the one he wanted, and when he was satisfied, he created Adam. It's not so hard to accept."

"Okay, I get it. So, now we have Adam, and God needs a place to put him, so he created the Garden of Eden."

"Exactly."

"And then he decided that Adam needed a companion, so he created Eve, from a rib of Adam."

"Really? Do you honestly believe that?"

"Of course."

"Okay. I'm not going to dispute or change the Scriptures, but you're going to have to start accepting the entire concept of Symbolism."

"What symbolism?"

"Symbolism is a way to take something that happened and make it seem that it happened a different way to make the story more spiritual."

"God didn't take a rib from Adam?"

"It doesn't matter. If you want to believe that God took a rib from Adam to create Eve, then so be it."

"Look, I'm pretty new at this acceptance of everything you say. Maybe I'm not so good with this *eyes wide open* approach."

"You'll be fine. The most important point here is that you now have a Man and a Woman, and they are naked, by human standards, because clothes haven't been invented. It was truly the Age of Innocence."

"Now, that makes sense."

"Happy to hear it."

"So we have two perfect human beings doing what?"

"Doing nothing. So, God started experimenting with different things to make them relate more to one another."

"Like what?"

"For starters he gave them the power to think and to reason. To apply logic, even when there weren't any situations yet to apply it to."

"Is this where you came in?"

"Yes, but don't get ahead of me. There I was, home for the holidays, and assuming my position as, *the elephant in the room....*"

"What holidays?"

"It was just an expression. Actually, I was there to hear the update on Adam and Eve."

"And?"

"God, Michael, and Gabriel were thrilled at the creation of Adam and Eve, because they were a non-heavenly species, yet still perfect in every way. And then, off handedly, I said, 'They only appear perfect. If given the chance, they would say No, just like I did.'"

"Oh, that must have gone over really well."

"It angered my father to no end. So, I said, 'the only way they will remain perfect and obedient, is if you don't allow them to be anything else. If you were to make them imperfect, meaning having the ability to choose for themselves, they will defy you.' And then the arguments started, with all of them saying that no being of any kind would abandon a perfect existence, even if given the choice.

But I challenged God to allow it to happen, to prove my point. I argued that if God gave Adam and Eve the freedom to choose, even with the threat of losing their perfection and innocence, that they would do it."

"And?"

"And what? Anyone with an IQ above a Googolplex should have known that Man was flawed from the moment God gave them the power to think and to reason. And, to apply logic, even when there weren't any situations yet to apply it to, as soon as they had these abilities, anything and everything about their perfectness was no longer valid."

"What's a Googolplex?"

"The biggest number of human comprehension, though for Man it's more theoretical than actual"

"I'll take your world for it. Explain to me how God could create something that was flawed, if it was created in his own image?"

"Again, don't confuse reality and symbolism. God created Man in the image he created, but it wasn't his *own* image. Especially when he created Eve. All you have to do is think about God creating Eve and it'll immediately become clearer."

"Then what happened?"

"God sent Gabriel down to tell Adam and Eve that God was making additions to the Garden, to include a Tree of Knowledge. Remember- symbolism, symbolism, symbolism, which all seem to accept that it was an apple tree, but that the fruit was not to be picked and certainly not to be eaten. Adam and Eve happily agreed, keeping in mind that eating was a foreign concept anyway. They didn't need to eat or drink. To make this more to your teachings, '...You are free to eat from any tree in the garden; but you must not eat from the tree of the knowledge of good and evil, for when you eat of it you will surely die.' (NIV, Genesis 2:15-17)."

"I went down to the Garden and checked Adam and Eve out. Adam was...Adam. But Eve, even before the first bite, was showing signs of being a flawed woman, in that she was the first example of Vanity, which is the deadly sin known as Pride."

"I take it this is when you showed up as the Serpent."

"We've already had this discussion. I did not show up as a serpent. I showed up as another Man."

"Didn't that freak them out?"

"No. Even though they didn't know me from Adam, they were happy to see me."

Chelsea almost wished that Lucifer could feel pain at this point.

"Once I had her in my confidence, I might have let it slip that there were some interesting things to be gained by eating from the Tree of Knowledge. Eve asked me, 'Like, what?'"

"Oh you must have loved watching this unfold."

"I told the truth. 'Pleasure, which you will experience if you can get Adam to also take a bite; that he will lust for you, and that the lust will make him vulnerable, and submissive to all of your wants and needs.' You have to remember- Eve was an afterthought. Adam was the true apple of God's eye."

"God, I hate you sometimes."

"Ohhh, 'sometimes' means you're actually starting to like me."

"Please continue."

"Eve looked at the fruit on the tree, and with her new power of knowledge, saw that it looked fresh and delicious. So, she picked the fruit and ate it. And then she gave some to Adam to eat, too. And then all Hell broke loose around the Garden. They realized, for the first time, that they were not wearing any clothes!"

"Well, at least they didn't die."

"Not right away. But at that point, a point that is left out of the story, they became mortal. So, yes, eventually they died."

"What happened before they died?"

"For starters, with the knowledge of nakedness, and embarrassment, Eve went shopping, trying on this leaf and that leaf from different trees, and then, when she tried covering herself with a grape leaf it was as if she had found the perfect wedding dress."

"Can't you be serious about anything?"

"There'll be plenty of time to be serious, as you are about to find out."

"Basically, from there, the story kept to the Scriptures?"

"More or less. But one thing that bore out, and that the Scriptures don't talk about, is that, It wasn't the apple on the tree that caused all of the problems. It was the pair on the ground...I always liked that one."

"You couldn't resist, could you?

"This is one of those times when I love being me."

"I don't care about you. I want to know more about the beginnings of Man, meaning Adam and Eve."

"Fine. Be that way. What else do you want to know?"

"The fact that Eve showed that kind of strength might make one to believe that Eve was the first example of the old expression, "Behind every great man is a woman.""

"Here's an interesting bit of trivia. Did you know that she actually coined the phrase?"

"I don't believe you."

"Cross my heart and hope to die."

"You can't die. And I don't want to give you any more lead-ins for your jokes."

"Aw, c'mon, just this once. Ask me what my answer was when she said that."

Chelsea hemmed and hawed, in her mind, debating if hearing his obvious forthcoming joke was worth asking to hear it. She finally succumbed.

"Fine. What was your answer?"

"I told her that the second part of the phrase should be, "And behind every destroyed man is the *same* woman.""

"How sexist of you."

"Hey, don't kill the messenger. If you seriously look at the events, you'll see that I didn't *force* Eve to take the first bite. I only *seduced* her into taking the first bite, by suggesting how good it tasted. She made the choice on her own. Had I taken the apple and *forced* her to take a bite, then you would have an argument. When you force someone to do something, against their free will, then it is most definitely, EVIL. But that was obviously not the case."

Chelsea didn't immediately respond, realizing that it would have been difficult to argue with his explanation. "In the meantime, can we please, finish the Garden story and move on?"

"And then shortly thereafter, we had the first example of true EVIL, when Cain killed Abel. That, was EVIL in its purest form. And I did not suggest it, or coerce him into doing it, in any way, shape, or form. He decided to kill his brother all on his own. It was the EVIL inside of every man, that most are able to suppress, that overcame him and caused him to commit that terrible act."

"And he was sent to Hell for doing it?"

"A beeline, as the expression goes."

"Why did God let that happen?"

"It was God's first test and acceptance of simply letting Nature take its course. It happened, and from that point God decided to just let Man, be Man - good, bad, or indifferent."

"So where do we go from here? What is God's plan for me?"

"I'm honestly not sure. For starters, what exactly were your thoughts when I told you the why and the how of your death?"

"Disbelief...anger...wanting revenge that the NEW WORLD ORDER did it to me and my family. And to the entire world for that matter."

"That must be it. The revenge part."

"Is that why I wasn't allowed to go right to Heaven? Because I still had anger and the wanting of revenge flowing through my veins?"

"That has to be it, or at least part of it. Is that what you want to do? Go back and get revenge?"

"I'd love it. But it's not likely that God would allow it."

"How do you know? Hmmm, maybe we could call it something else."

"I can see your thoughts spinning, but I'm not sure what's going on."

"I'm looking for a synonym for "revenge" in the Book of Dinosaurs."

"I'd hate to think I'm insulting God, but does insanity run in your family?"

"Most definitely not. Why would you ask such a thing?"

"Because you said you're looking for a synonym for "revenge" in the Book of Dinosaurs."

"Oh, that. I was just amusing myself with a play on words. When you were on Earth, and looking for a synonym, didn't you also use a, *The...saurus*?"

Chelsea just shook her head in disbelief, knowing that Traveler's word games were part of the package of having him help. Nonetheless, knowing her thoughts by his ability to read them, was not a deterrent.

"You have no idea how much fun it really is, being me."

"I'll take your word for it. Just tell me. Is it possible to go back?"

"It's been done before. But I can tell you from experience, without a well-forged plan of how you would do it, God isn't about to even consider it."

"Wanting revenge isn't enough?"

"Definitely not. Not in the form of physical violence that is. If it is, then God will never go for it. As a matter of fact, if that's your motive, you may end up spending more time here than your Uncle Joey."

"I don't need to physically hurt anyone to exact revenge."

"Then you had better decide what kind of revenge you're talking about, or you're going nowhere. God isn't big on wasting time on lost causes, especially lost causes the second time around."

"Then show me the way."

"I can't. This has to be your idea and your quest. To do anything other than that would take an act of God."

"You trying to be funny, again?"

"No, I'm serious. I don't think he'd be very happy that I would even ask to help. It has taken me eons just for him to take my calls, and then to ask this?"

"But you haven't said no, so why not try? How do you call him?"

"Um, you know. Just look up and say…Hi, got time to talk?"

"And?"

"If he wants to talk, he'll talk. If not, he'll ignore me."

"How often do you call?"

"The usual. Christmas, Easter, Birthdays."

"God has a birthday?"

"I don't think there is one, specific day. In a way, every day is his birthday. It's just kind of a running joke that whenever I call, I wish him a Happy Birthday."

"Did you ever buy him a gift?"

"What could I possibly give to someone who has everything?"

"An apology might be a good start."

"Forget about it."

"So, you've never asked God for a favor since he cast you out?"

"Nope. Never."

"Then let's take a different approach. Did God ever ask *you* to do him a favor, seeing as if he told you to do something, you would have simply said, No.

"Well, there was this one time."

"When?"

"It's a long story."

"Like I have somewhere else to go?"

"Okay, okay. Everyone was mad at me for messing with Moses. I honestly didn't mean any harm by it, but he was such a Boy Scout. He could have qualified for merit badges the world would never understand. I tempted him here, tempted him there, and true to form, he rebuked my temptations at every turn. He was just, so… Good."

"You tried to tempt Moses and he refused? What did you expect?"

"I was hoping that maybe, just one time, he would have taken some joy in accepting an opportunity to stray from his perfect life."

"So, what happened?"

"Well, Moses started praying for help from God, and God, in turn, asked me to intercede, knowing that bringing on the ten plagues would be to my liking. Watching Pharoah deal with the plagues was one of the most fun-times in my life on Earth. For the record, Pharoah was an EVIL man.

Chelsea looked at him questioningly---

"*You* sent the ten plagues?"

"What, you don't believe me?"

"I'm not so sure. Was, that it?"

"No, there was also the parting of the Red Sea."

"You expect me to believe that you did that also?"

"Well, God actually did it. I was just the trigger-man so to speak."

"I think you make this stuff up as you go along."

"I don't have to make anything up. Just remember the immortal words of the Father of American Literature, Mark Twain- *'Truth is stranger than fiction.'*"

"All right. At this point I'm willing to hear anything. But please, just the short version."

"Simply, Moses fled from Pharoah with a bunch of others and was about to get caught. Michael had already been sent to help, but Michael was only helping as a rear guard, making '... a pillar of cloud, which generally led the people through the desert, wrapped itself around them from behind, protecting them from Egyptian arrows and projectiles. At the same time, the pillar of fire illuminated the night for the people of Israel.'

Again, when it comes to the Old Testament, you really should go to the original source. The Hebrew version is very accurate."

"Just finish the story."

"Moses and his followers suddenly found themselves at the shores of the Red Sea and nowhere to go. They were definitely trapped. But here was the problem, and you know God. He knew what was going to happen and still didn't intercede, beyond sending Michael. Personally, I liked Moses, so I asked God what I could do to help. He said to me, 'You have the power to help. If you want to help him, help him. I won't stand in your way.'"

"And?"

"'And,' means, Moses called on God to help him part the waters to escape, and God told him to, '...And you raise your staff and stretch out your hand over the sea and split it, and the children of Israel shall come in the midst of the sea on dry land...And the Egyptians shall know that I am the Lord, when I will be glorified through Pharaoh, through his chariots, and through his horsemen.' All that God meant by that was that the miracle of the parting sea and the escape of the Israelites would send a clear message to Pharoah that the Israelites were God's chosen people."

"So where did you come in?"

"God told me to help Moses, but make it look good. When Moses raised his staff, I also raised mine, and the waters parted. Oh, by the way. This is the same staff."

Traveler was referring to the staff that he was carrying when he met Chelsea for the first time, and was still carrying with him.

"Remember when I said, 'If I believe that *my* staff is *thy* staff, and that *thy* staff is *his* staff...?' Now do you get it?"

Chelsea was still trying to absorb the new-found version of Moses escaping Pharoah.

"For the umpteenth time, if you really want to know, you have to go to the version that hasn't been played with since it was written. You have to read the Hebrew version, and when it comes to their religion, Jews don't lie, especially keeping in mind that Moses was the most famous Jew, ever…well, until Jesus showed up."

"Either way, I'm glad it all turned out the way it did."

"Yeah, me too."

Chelsea decided to test Traveler a bit.

"Side note- Charlton Heston as Moses, or the real Moses?"

"Definitely Heston… Moses would have never joined the NRA and you're going to need the NRA to defeat the NEW WORLD ORDER."

"This conversation is exhausting. When do we sleep?"

"We don't. There's no need for it."

"How about breaks? You know, like, to take a walk, read a book. Just some 'me' time?"

"Go ahead. Maybe you'll come up with an idea that will convince God you should have a chance at going back and getting that revenge."

"How long was I gone?"

"How long did it seem?"

"I'm not sure. You know, it's almost as if I never left."

"You didn't. But you'll get used to it. You're going to find that the hereafter is a lot different than what you were used to as a mortal on Earth. Time is not measurable. Did you come up with a plan?"

"I think I have. I must have run a hundred scenarios around in my head until I finally landed on the right one. If God will allow me to go back, I'll write a book, using what I already saw and experienced, to warn the people of pending doom if they don't stop the forces of EVIL from taking control. What do you think?"

"It sounds like a plan, if you can get people to read it. But you've never written a book before. And what you know about the forces of EVIL, meaning the NEW WORLD ORDER and the DEMOCRATIC PARTY wouldn't even scratch the surface of what you need to tell."

"But is it a plan that God will go for?"

"It's not for me to say."

"Then how do I ask him?"

"You already have."

"No I haven't. I haven't even met him, yet."

"Chelsea, he is all knowing. That includes all hearing. He's heard every word you have thought or spoken since you took your first breath as a newborn."

"Well, I haven't got all day to wait for an answer. If I'm going to write a book, I need to get started right now."

"He wants to know where you are going to get the information you need for the book?"

"I didn't hear God ask you anything?"

"He called on my private line. And in agreement with what I just said, He also said that you don't know enough about anything, to actually fill a book that anyone would find compelling enough to want to help you change the course of history, meaning the future."

"Is there a course available anywhere that will teach me what I need to know?"

"You could *ghost* a class at a university back on Earth, but that could take years, in Earth time."

"Was that another joke?"

"Chelsea, please, what do you take me for?"

"That's it! I'll get a private tutor. You can be my tutor. I mean, who knows more about Man, Earth, and EVIL than you. You're perfect!"

"Wow, all of this, *damned if I do, damned if I don't* stuff is finally catching up with me.

"Yeah, penance can be very demanding sometimes."

Chelsea suddenly got very excited at the possibility of actually going back.

"I'm going to get a second chance! This is incredible! God is going to let me go back to Earth as an angel to fight EVIL."

"No, it doesn't work that way. First of all, you won't be an angel. God won't do that. If He wanted a simple solution he could wave his hand and be done with EVIL. But that's not God's plan for Man. Man has to fend for himself. And that means you will also have to fend for yourself."

"That's doesn't make a lot of sense to me."

"What you don't know about God and Heaven would fill...bibles. God is not there to solve the problems of Man, especially when Man created the problems. God's solution is to reward Man, once Man figures it out and does something about it, and once he has done that, his reward will be having eternal life in Heaven. Remember, you already had that chance, and you failed miserably. As a matter of fact, half of the population failed."

"I tried."

"Since when is sending out a bunch of emails and Tweets called *fighting*? Did you sue anyone? Write a blog? Write a book? Hold a rally or a march? What exactly did you do?"

Chelsea thought about it for a moment, and then dropped her head in embarrassment, knowing that Traveler was right.

"It wouldn't have done me any good. I wrote a tweet criticizing the teaching of Critical Race Theory and they fired me."

"Mmm, not really."

"I think I ought to know if I was fired or not."

"Oh, you were certainly fired, but not for posting the tweet."

"Was to."

"Didn't they give you a chance to take down the tweet and apologize? Better yet, to grovel and publicly beg for forgiveness for your shortsightedness and irresponsible tweet?"

Again, Chelsea had to think about her answer.

"I guess. What's the difference? I still got fired."

"For an educated person, you are dense. They didn't care that you wrote the tweet. As a matter of fact, you did them a favor. You publicly volunteered to expose yourself and the other teachers who got your tweet and didn't criticize you for writing it. But you absolutely were not fired for writing it. You were fired for not apologizing and begging for forgiveness; for not *falling into line* and promising to only speak when spoken to, and then to only support the TEACHER'S UNION narrative and propaganda. That's why you were fired."

"I never thought about it that way."

"You will, now. The truth hurts, doesn't it? Even for you."

Chelsea emersed herself into deep thought and consideration of Traveler's condemnation of her inactions when it came to condemning or challenging the actions of anything that was part of the NEW WORLD ORDER takeover.

"You're right...You know, you're so much better at this than I am. I never thought about people that I worked with, meaning the teachers union, doing everything to take me down behind my back."

"You need to understand the modern concept of unions, and who controls them. Whereas, in the beginning, unions were a great way to fight the EVILs of the owners of factories who were enslaving their workers, the problem is that every union ever formed eventually ceded power to a few, and then the union members simply went along with the hierarchy and let them do whatever they wanted, as long as the members kept getting higher wages, perks, and retirement benefits. They simply became the MOB. You do realize that your union, the California Teacher's Union was one of the biggest defenders of the NEW WORLD ORDER policies and propaganda that there was. Did you ever seriously look at what they did to the education system? They stole your kids out from under you, poisoned their minds, and created robots that they wouldn't have to ever worry about."

"Not with the friends I had."

"Maybe so, but next time you look in the mirror, just remember that it's you, you are seeing, and not David with a sling."

"Did that really happen?"

"Absolutely. You know, I taught him how to use the sling."

"Of course you did."

Chelsea had finally figured out that Traveler would take credit for just about anything that ever happened on Earth. After all, who could possibly question him? Assuming that Chelsea had accepted his latest brag, he simply moved onto his next thought.

"Which brings us to the fork in the road. Which way are you going?"

"I want you to show me where I went wrong; where everyone went wrong. And that will give me the knowledge I need to write the book I want to write. Do you think God will go for that?"

"You can ask him yourself."

In the blink of an eye Chelsea was now standing before God, who was seated on a gilded throne of opulence beyond her wildest, worldly imaginations. And as Traveler had alluded, God was in human form with a crown of jewels atop his long white hair, and his long white beard draping down over the long white robe that he wore. To his right sat Jesus, and sitting on the steps of the altar that the throne sat upon, were Michael and Gabriel.

"Welcome to Heaven."

"I'm really here? And you're really God?"

"Yes, you're really here, and Yes, I am really God."

"This is sooo cool…But I never saw St. Peter at the Gates of Heaven."

"He doesn't do that. St. Peter is only at the Gates greeting newcomers if it's the beginning of a joke."

"Ohhh. I see."

"Obviously, I am what you expected?"

"Perfect."

"Yes, I knew that. I find it usually works best to simply appear in the vision you had of me while you were on Earth."

"Isn't everyone's vision about the same?"

"Pretty much. Oh, and just for the record, these are my three sons; (pointing) Michael, Gabriel, and Jesus, who, as you have been told, sits at my right hand."

"It's very nice to meet all of you. Now that I'm dead, and I'm here in Heaven, does that make me an angel?"

"Not quite. For now, let's just say, angel-in-training."

"When I actually become an angel, do I get a halo and wings?"

"I know this is going to disappoint you, but they're not a real thing. Halos and wings are a Renaissance take on angels."

"Ohhh, you're right. I'm so disappointed."

"Yes, I knew you would be, but we all have our cross to bear."

God casually looked over at Jesus, who, under his breath, commented, "Don't I know it."

Without hesitation she jumped into her next comment.

"I have a million questions."

"Actually, you only have 33, and you've already used five."

"You know that I only have 33?"

"You *do* know to whom you are talking, don't you?"

"Oh, yeah, you know what I am going to ask because you're all knowing and all seeing."

"Well, it's good to know you were paying attention in Sunday School. Then again, I knew that also."

"So, why do I have to ask the questions if you already know what I'm going to ask?"

"Because, whereas I know the questions and the answers, you don't. Now, do you see why you have to *ask* the questions?"

"Ohhh, so I can hear each answer before asking the next question."

"Lucifer said you were a quick study."

"You talked to Traveler, I mean, Lucifer?"

"No."

"But you just said that Lucifer said I was a quick study."

"Yes."

"But if you haven't talked to him, how did you know he said it?"

"Because I heard him say it to you. You seem to quickly forget that I am God."

"Oh my God, I'm so sorry. This is going to take a bit to get used to."

"Yes, I know."

Chelsea started to laugh.

"I am *so* going to enjoy working with you. Excuse me. *For you.*"

"Yes, I know. I'll take your tenth question, now."

"I told Traveler that I wished that I had a second chance to do the right thing - to go back and give it another try. And Traveler said he wasn't sure if it's possible. Or that it might be possible, but that maybe you wouldn't allow me to do it unless I had a solid plan with good reasons for wanting to do so."

"That's not a question."

"Oh. Can I go back?"

"Why would you want to go back, when it took so much to get here?"

"To help fight EVIL."

"That's a pretty broad answer. What do you think you could do, if given the chance, that you didn't do the first time around?"

"I know that the EVIL intentions of the NEW WORLD ORDER and the DEMOCRATIC PARTY were actually happening right in front of my eyes and that I did nothing about it. No one did, because we weren't aware that it was happening. I'd like to think that if I could use my second chance to go back and spread the word that we could stop EVIL in its tracks. You know, maybe use the Sword of Gideon, or something."

"Okay, for starters, Gideon, who by the way asked the same thing you are, meaning to go back, which I allowed because he had a plan, never used a sword. That whole sword thing was in the imagination of a Hollywood writer."

"But Gideon went back to save his people, didn't he?"

"Yes."

"Then, there you have it. It's possible to go back. I want to do the same."

"He had a plan. You don't. No plan, no go."

"Then, send Michael or Gabriel with me. They have swords."

"More Renaissance images. Angels don't use swords."

"Then what am I to do? I need to go back."

"Think about it, come up with a plan, and then I'll seriously consider it. And not until."

"How many questions have I used up so far?"

"Including that one, thirteen."

"But you're God. You already know my plan."

"True. Except that *you* need to know your plan, and tell me your plan. And until you do that, so that I know it is *your* plan, and not *my* plan, then there is no plan. And if there is no plan, then there is no chance of you being reborn."

"Why would you let EVIL win?"

"I am not letting EVIL win. *Man* is letting EVIL win. Let me rephrase. Man *let* EVIL win, which is how you got here in the first place. GOOD must *fight* its own battles, and *win* its own battles. I knew it had to be this way since Eve took a bite of the fruit from the Tree of Knowledge. So, come up with a plan."

"How much time do I have?"

"All the time in Heaven. So, take your time."

Chelsea smiled. "That was pretty clever. You took the expression, *All the time in the world*, and made it, *All the time in Heaven*. Now I see where Traveler gets it."

"You *do* know how this works don't you? And thinking that Lucifer is a chip off the old block is not winning you any points."

"Oh, my God. I'm so sorry."

"Yes. I know. Apology accepted."

Though she actually had no reference of time, and being the *new kid in Heaven*, coming up with a solid plan to convince God that she was worthy of a return to Earth to get people to notice her, to listen to her, and to help her deliver the message that would defeat EVIL on Earth, was a daunting task. She finally came up with the idea of writing a book, with all of the messages that she needed to convey as a single source. Once back on earth, she would publish the book and hope that she had written the book well enough to grab the attention of the masses, who would join her in the war against EVIL.

"I've got it! Okay, the pen is mightier than the sword. Right?"

"In a war of words, yes. In a war of battles, not so much."

"Well, I'm hardly Joan of Arc, so I'm convinced my only choice is words. I'd like to go back, write a book about everything I know that happened, and try and change the course of history in the battle of GOOD versus EVIL."

"To what end?"

"To end EVIL, and to prove that Man, when given the right tools and the right motivation will do the right thing."

"And how exactly do you plan to get this knowledge you'll need for the book?"

"From you?"

"No, because if I do it, it will automatically happen, and I've already told you that it has to be your plan and your book."

"But I'm going to need help."

"I'll make a deal with you, which really isn't a deal, because, contrary to popular belief, I don't make deals."

"Okay...but I happen to know that the reward of Heaven only goes to those who live a life of GOOD. Isn't that a deal?"

"Very good. You see, I let you come up with that all on your own, which is proof to me that you can do this."

"In that case, I'm going to go with my second choice. Traveler."

Jesus couldn't resist reverting back to his time on Earth to interject his questioning of using Lucifer to help her. "OY VEY!"

Hearing Jesus' comment, God asked what he meant by it. "Do you have something you'd like to add?"

"You would actually allow Lucifer to teach her what she has to know? At any point he could sabotage the whole operation just for kicks."

Chelsea was quick to come to Traveler's defense.

"I don't agree. Traveler has shown that he can be a good friend, and an honest friend. I know he'll do the right thing."

God turned to Michael for his opinion. "Michael?"

"Well, he came through for Moses. One time out of a few gazillion chances, at least shows promise."

God then completed the process by asking Gabriel's opinion.

"Gabriel?"

"I hate to blow my own horn, or sit in judgement of my own brother, but I'm with Michael on this one. I vote that we give Lucifer a chance to prove himself."

God turned to Jesus, who still hadn't actually cast his vote.

"I'm still not happy with Lucifer making my life on Earth his personal mischief mission. As a human being of the times I sometimes still get seasick thinking about that storm he created."

"And, you calmed the seas and saved your disciples."

Jesus was softening a bit, but suddenly, the prankster side of Traveler emerged in the recounting of another incident while Jesus walked on Earth as Man.

"Yeah, I guess that in the end it turned out alright. But how about when he showed up at my Brit Milah posing as a blind, octogenarian, Mohel, with a bad case of palsy? I thought Joseph was going to have a heart attack."

Michael and Gabriel start to laugh.

Michael immediately verbalized his thoughts. "Now that was funny. If it had actually happened, I was waiting for Joseph, a carpenter by trade, to be giving instructions. 'Now remember, measure twice and cut once!'"

Jesus was quick to respond. "He was blind! How was he going to measure?"

God interceded to stop the bickering. "Enough. There will be no more discussion about that. If Lucifer had actually gone through with it, there might be something to talk about, but it never happened, so let's move on."

God now needed Jesus' vote. "Jesus, what say you?"

"Fine. Let Lucifer help her."
"Then we are in agreement. What is your plan for the book?"

Chelsea was now reinvigorated and excited that the vote had confirmed her wish to go back.

"I want **to go back to** the year 2024. It's the most critical election in the fight against the NEW WORLD ORDER, the DEMOCRATIC PARTY, and the JOE BIDEN AGENDA. It's so clear that if the NEW WORLD ORDER, the DEMOCRATIC PARTY win the election, we already know, that from there it was basically over for good, for GOOD."

God, in an earthly way, smiled. "That sounds like a good plan."

"But I have another concern. I don't have a title for the book yet. Or, what name to publish it under. I can't be me, or people who knew me will be too confused to believe anything I have to say."

"Tell you what. You concentrate on the actual writing of the book, and I'll come up with your name. How's that?"

"Deal. What will my name be?"

"When the time comes, I will have John baptize you and give you your new name."

"I'm going to be baptized by John the Baptist?"

"Absolutely. He'd love to do it. Take my word for it. You'll be baptized and reborn by the hands of John the Baptist."

"What age should I go back as? The same age as I was in 2024, or the age I was when I came to Heaven?"

"It's your plan."

"I think the older version of me. I think that with a little bit of age on my face, people won't be so quick to dismiss me."

"Okay, but you can't be going back as you."

"I don't understand."

"You can't very well go back as yourself in 2024. There would be two of you."

"Can't you just make us into one person?"

"I could, but I won't. You lived out your life, and then you died in 2036. That is how you shall be entered into the Book of Good."

"Oh... Then how can I do what I want to do?"

"You're going to go back as you, but in another body. Everyone who comes in contact with you won't know it's actually you. They will think you are a different person."

"Who will I be?"

"You will go back as the name you will be baptized as."

"So, I will always be me, but in the body of this, new person?"

"Exactly. Do you understand?"

"Not really."

"Did you ever see the movie *Heaven Can Wait*, with Warren Beatty?... No, you didn't."

"How do you know I never saw it?"

"I thought by now that you'd be done asking that question, though I knew it would be one of **the thirty-three.**"

"Sorry."

"Just take my word for it. You'll understand it when you come back to Heaven and get the DVD. The Warren Beatty version is actually much better than the original."

"You can rent DVDs in Heaven? Oh, let me guess. When Blockbuster died it came to Heaven."

"No. But when Blockbuster died, if you had bought Netflix, you would have been a millionaire, overnight."

"Yeah, I was never that lucky. How many movies are available?"

"Eight hundred thousand, seventy-three, to include straight-to-video and made-for-television."

"Oh my God, it would take a lifetime to see all of them."

"Actually, no lifetime would be enough. Not even Methuselah. But luckily, when you finally get to Heaven, permanently, it won't be an issue."

"Wow. I love movies. How does it work?"

"All you have to do is simply think what you'd like to see and it appears. Popcorn is available for the asking."

"We can get popcorn in Heaven?"

"Of course. It's a perk for making it to Heaven. And it's non-GMO."

"Extra butter?"

"Absolutely. And it's organic."

"Wow. Non-GMO popcorn and organic butter. This is like… Heaven."

God and his sons exchange glances with one another, at hearing what sounds like the musings of a teenager.

Gabriel verbalized his thoughts. "Is she serious?"

Michael mused, "Maybe we should take a second vote."

God ended the back-and-forth with, "No. A promise is a promise."

God then turned to Chelsea and asked, "Anything else?"

"Yes. There is one question that has really been bugging me for years, and I promised myself that I would ask you when I met you… *Where Was Your Wrath When We Needed It?*"

"If you ever finish your book and publish it, I promise that you'll get your answer. Just keep in mind that God works in mysterious ways."

Chelsea mulled-over God's answer, not really sure what it meant.

"Wow, this has been great. Now, all I have to do is come up with a catchy title."

"I'm sure that won't be a problem."

"I have one more question. When I go back, and if I am successful, will it actually change history?

"Actually, it will automatically begin to change the future. But changing everything is a double-edged sword. At first, your problem is to convince people that you should be listened to, and that the facts in your book should make any reasonably intelligent person conclude that BIDEN, or anyone endorsed by the NEW WORLD ORDER and the DEMONIC PARTY should be ignored and defeated. The problem is this - the Butterfly Effect, as they liked to call it back in 2024. From the first time and day that someone reads your book, history will immediately begin to change, meaning altering the future course of history. If one person, especially if that is a person or persons of influence, makes a change from what he, or she, originally did, it begins. It could mean that your recounting of events that actually happened will no longer happen, and they will try to use that against you. Be prepared."

"Yeah, I'm having a little bit of a problem wrapping my arms around this, because I already know what happens as a result of the NEW WORLD ORDER, the DEMOCRATIC PARTY, and JOE BIDEN stealing the 2024 presidential election."

"You just do what you're going back to do, and if you're successful...well, again, you just let me worry about the outcome and how it will affect the future. Anything else?"

"But no matter what, I'm on my own?"

"Yes."

A giant grin emerged over Chelsea's angelic face. "Then, I guess it's time to go back...But you already knew that..."

Chelsea suddenly found herself back in the Garden of Eden. She wandered around until she found Traveler sitting on a mound of grass under the Tree of Knowledge, eating an apple.

"I've been expecting you."

"I'm still trying to get used to this being-dead-thing, and time without time. How long was I gone?"

"It's like you never left."

"I have good news. God is going to let me go back."

"Yes, I know."

"Let me guess...a little bird told you."

"God uses doves. You know, it's that whole symbolism thing of a dove being the messengers of God, and love and peace. Care for a bite?"

"No, thank you. You disappointed me."

"How so?

"You said you'd be there when I asked God, 'Where was your wrath when we needed it?'"

"I was there."

"I didn't see you."

"I didn't want to get Junior all riled up any more than usual, after his recounting of the Bris."

"Oh, that. I have to admit, that was pretty...."

"Funny?"

"I'll leave it to the family to decide."

"But, to answer your question, I was there, but observing from the, *wings*."

"Don't you ever get tired of the word-play?"

"Never. So, how can I be of service?"

"Do you type?"

"A million words a minute. Even on a manual."

"No, seriously."

"I was being serious, but we won't need a typewriter until the book is finished. Have you put much thought into this, or are you going to run with it and see where you end up?"

"No, I have definitely been thinking about it. For starters, I need to know everything that I obviously missed on my first try."

"Starting when?"

"You mean, like the beginning? Here, in the Garden?"

Traveler gestured that the beginning would be where they were, right there in the Garden of Eden.

"No, I'm pretty clear on all of that. I've decided that I have to concentrate on the 2020 presidential election for the beginning of my book. As I recall, that's when EVIL finally got its firm grip on the world as I knew it, and began on making it Hell on Earth. But I'd also like to get your perspective on a lot of other things, too."

"What do you want to know?"

Traveler suddenly held up his finger, gesturing that Chelsea should hold her thought. Traveler looked upward. In what seemed like a brief moment, he finally dropped his head to look at her.

"Okay, continue."

"You know, these messages you keep getting from God are very distracting. And not nice. Weren't you raised better, to know that whispering and telling secrets in public is rude?"

"Hellooo. It was God!"

"Well, that shouldn't matter."

"Okay. I get it. It was God. I apologize. He just wanted to give me the rules."

"Rules?"

"Yes, rules. There are always rules. I'm to show you, and guide you; point you in the right direction but not push you to go there. I can't divulge anything I know unless it is in direct correlation to whatever questions you ask. My role will be to play the Devil's Advocate."

"So, where do we start?"

"With Rule #1."

"What is it?"

Traveler was taking great pride in his role as Chelsea's teacher in her first foray into writing, in what would become an expose' on the NEW WORLD ORDER and its destruction of Man and Planet Earth. With Traveler's knowledge of world history, he could have helped her write a twenty-three-volume set of encyclopedias, but he knew that it wouldn't have done her any good to have that much knowledge and facts.

"Rule #1 - If you are going to write this book, it must be truthful in its information and teachings, to the core. Everything in the book must be factual, and verifiable by the average person with a simple search on their computer, or in 2024, the *touch of the screen* on their cell phone."

"I haven't even decided what I should write, and already I'm worried that no one will listen, no matter what I write."

"It's a legitimate concern. If I would have any advice, whatsoever, it would be to control the depth of the narrative."

"What exactly does that mean?"

"I can think of a dozen instances in your lifetime where there were many who believed that *more* is better, believing that no one could ever argue or disagree with a million facts. Here's the problem with that kind of thinking. If you give someone too many facts, they will ignore them, because the average person, in and of your time, was too lazy to read them, or even hear them. And here is another problem. Seemingly *irrefutable evidence*, is not *proof*. And here is where you are going to run into your biggest challenge. You cannot, nor will God allow you, to utilize the NEW WORLD ORDER, DEMOCRATIC PARTY, or the JOE BIDEN ADMINISTRATION's favorite form of propaganda, in the times of when you will be going back. I'm specifically referring to the practice of the "Wrap-up Smear.""

"Fine. I can certainly live with that. But now that you've mentioned it, what ever happened to Nancy Pelosi? I honestly don't remember."

"That's because she had outlived her usefulness and disappeared from the political arena by 2026. Then, she just slithered away, with no apology for the symbolic metaphor. Age finally caught up with what a small fortune in plastic surgery couldn't hide, and she died in 2027. On her way to Hell she kept screaming, 'But I'm a good person.' And, though a Catholic, she did not even get a whiff of Purgatory."

"God didn't forgive her?"

"For what? She wasn't repentant in the least, insisting all the while that she was Nancy Pelosi and how dare anyone criticize her for anything she had said or done. When she got to Hell, for her it was like a duck taking to water. She immediately installed herself into the role of Speaker of the Damned, and will stay in that position, forever."

"Damned or not, I feel sorry for her."

"Don't waste your time."

"I may as well ask. What happened to Joe Biden? He was also Catholic."

"Straight to Heaven."

"Heaven? Really? How is that possible after what he did?"

"God never holds the mentally impaired accountable for their actions, and with Joe it went all the way back to 2018. Up to that point he was looking at Purgatory. But when the NEW WORLD ORDER and the DEMOCRATIC PARTY came knocking, he lost all sense of right and wrong, or GOOD and EVIL. As a matter of fact, without the daily drug boost, during his campaign and right through his entire presidency, he was lucky to even know what day it was. So, Joe Biden got a pass."

"Interesting. In a way I wish he had gone to Hell also, but if God was good with it, then I guess I'm good with it."

"Joe doesn't know how lucky he was that it wasn't up to me."

Traveler was good with letting Chelsea digest everything he had been telling her. After all, she was technically still human, and therefore didn't digest and understand everything as quickly as she would someday be able to do, when she finally and eternally entered Heaven, and graduated to angel status.

"Before we move on, let me finish my point about *too much* being a dangerous route. Do you remember Mike Lindell?"

"The name is familiar, but no, I don't."

"The *My Pillow* guy with the moustache?"

"Oh yeah, I actually read his book. And I also loved his pillows and sheets."

"He spent millions of dollars and put together a video called "Absolute Proof," offering what he considered *irrefutable evidence* that the 2020 election had been stolen by Joe Biden."

"I remember that he didn't get very far with it, did he?"

"Unfortunately, no."

"What did you think of his video and proof?"

"100% spot-on. But he had two things going against him. First, it was so detailed and intricate that it was too difficult for the average person to take the time to read and understand it. Secondly, he didn't take into consideration that it wasn't Joe Biden he was up against. It was the NEW WORLD ORDER and the DEMOCRATIC PARTY, with resources and influence ten times greater than he could have ever imagined. The facts and evidence he was able to uncover made Mike Lindell the NEW WORLD ORDER and the DEMOCRATIC PARTY's biggest threat to exposing what they had done; even more than the entire Republican Party, so they set out to destroy him."

"They did, didn't they?"

"His evidence got destroyed by the lies and propaganda of the NEW WORLD ORDER, but Mike, true to form, had a strong faith in GOOD and ready to give it his all in the next battle, if given the chance. Hopefully, *you* will be that chance."

Luckily, Chelsea had been old enough to understand the implications of the last stand of GOOD vs. EVIL, and stand for that which she knew to be GOOD. Many on the side of GOOD had tried to awaken the masses from the propaganda-instilled stupor that had gotten control of the minds of most, thanks to the media and publicity arm of the NEW WORLD ORDER, which had used all of its might for years-on-end to convince the masses that the existence of the NEW WORLD ORDER, even in part, was an unproveable conspiracy theory cooked up by Conservatives, and was therefore nothing more than a myth. Yet, when the NEW WORLD ORDER publicly admitted to their existence in 2024, the leftist, do as you are told Mass Media and Social Media, ignored it.

"You may have benefitted from baring your soul to me, but, more than ever, I'm totally confused about GOOD vs. EVIL. If you claim that you're not the source of EVIL in the world, then who is?"

"Finally...finally someone has asked the right question. But it will be very difficult for you to understand, because it will go against everything you have ever been taught, or believed."

"Try me."

"For starters, I'm not the Devil here...Let me rephrase. I actually *am* the Devil here, but I'm not the one you have to worry about. Man has always been anxious to point the finger at me, to deflect from his own sins; to find a scapegoat. I'm sure you've heard the phrase, 'The Devil made me do it.' But I never made anyone do anything. All I ever needed to do was point out the two choices and let Man decide for himself. And that includes when Eve ate the apple. It was Eve, herself, who got Adam to take a bite. I had nothing to do with it."

"Are you trying to say that EVIL doesn't exist?"

"Oh, EVIL most definitely exists, and it is everywhere. But the first thing that you must understand is that EVIL is not a person. It is not Lucifer, or Satan, or the Devil. Simply put, it is not Me. What you have to grasp is that the true source of EVIL is Man, himself. Man is horribly flawed, meaning that Man is not born *Good*. Man is born...*vulnerable,* and spends his entire life striving to be *Good*. And no one knows that better than I, as I was there to see it all happen, firsthand, when Man, the first man, showed how weak and vulnerable he truly was. My tempting Eve to take the first bite wasn't evil. Eve getting Adam to take a bite wasn't evil. But when their first-born murdered his brother, that was EVIL in its purest form. Shall I continue?"

"Do I have a choice?"

"No. Man tries to fight and resist the temptations of EVIL, but eventually, when he sees that there isn't any reward in it for him, like money, power, a sexual conquest, or fame, to name a few, then he is happy to jump over the line and bask in the short-term pleasures derived from the sins he has committed. Most are able to jump back to the side of GOOD, and stay there. But as I have seen many times, there are too many who enjoy being evil so much that they have no desire to be anything else. They get twice the joy out of using evil to make the GOOD suffer from their deeds. I have just described the NEW WORLD ORDER, the DEMOCRATIC PARTY, and the BIDEN ADMINISTRATION that you will go up against in 2024."

Traveler watched as the wheels turned at high-speed in Chelsea's head. Hearing what Traveler had just said was not easy to accept, but then again, who would know better than he. But she remained defiant, still not convinced that everything he had said was gospel.

"You say that Man is born EVIL, and spends his entire life striving to be good. But isn't that because of you?"

Traveler was now experiencing the two-steps forward and one-step-backwards phenomenon in having Chelsea accept what Traveler considered to be simple precepts.

"How many times do I have to tell you that I've never been the cause of anything. You seem to be fixated on Scripture, so let me ask you this? Can you cite one instance, anywhere in the Bible where I, personally, committed an EVIL act?"

Chelsea's countenance clearly showed her mind, scanning the Scriptures that she had committed to memory, but she didn't have an answer.

"Let me save you the time and effort to find an evil act in the Bible, that is attributed to me. You won't find one. As a matter of fact, if I gave you the time to do so, you will just confuse yourself even more, as the Scriptures, that you so-adhere to, don't even agree with one another. Ezekial and Isaiah, from the Old Testament, being two obsessives with my fall from Heaven don't agree with Revelations in the New Testament about the how and why of Dear Old Dad throwing me out of Heaven. Not only do Matthew, Mark, Luke, and John all vary from one another, but all four have had to share the spotlight so that Man, throughout the ages could pick which one he liked more. Doesn't that alone, give you pause?"

Traveler was on a roll, and knowing he had a captive audience, went into hyperdrive to get his message across.

"And to complicate things, the Old Testament was written in Ancient Hebrew. And then, around the time that the books of the New Testament were being written, the Ancient Hebrew was translated into Modern Hebrew, which was then translated into Ancient Greek, and then into Latin. In 1611 King James decided that the Latin version needed to be in English, and then that version was translated and rewritten 270 years later by a bunch of scholars who spent more time arguing if American English was as good as British English, and since that rewrite, another 30,000 permanent changes have been made here and there by more scholars. The point of all of this history, is, why would you sit there and tell me that you know who and what I am, based on the King James of modern times which has been rewritten tens of thousands of times? Which brings us to that point in our discussion, where you, as an angel-in-training must come to grips with many things. For starters there is a big difference between *fact* and *faith*, when it comes to the Bible, as you know it."

"But the Bible is the *Word of God*, and therefore factual."
"Okay, let's take a different approach? Which version, and in which language, are we talking about?"

Again, Chelsea honestly didn't have an answer.

"Let me get something clear. I am not here to question or destroy your faith, or any conceptions you may have of God's existence and his eternal plan for Man. Based on faith it is all intact, exactly as you have always believed. I am merely trying to point out that your beliefs in who and what "*I*" am, are based on the writings of men, not the word of God. If I were the Prince of Darkness, as opposed to the Prince of Heaven that some have also described me as being in their writings, do you honestly think that God would have entrusted me with helping you to achieve your goal?"

Obviously, Traveler was making some very valid points, but to give into him was, nonetheless, contrary to her education of God and Man.

"Hellooo...That was not a rhetorical question!"
"Alright, I get the point! You're not a Serpent. You're a Man...sort of. And not Evil."
"Well, it's a start. Just remember that Man believes in God because of Faith. And as they say, *Faith can move mountains...* Matthew 17:20 in case you were wondering."

"I suppose you were the one who gave Jesus the idea of saying it?"

"No, actually, he thought of that one on his own."

"How generous of you."

Traveler took the opportunity to reinforce his position with scriptural evidence of support.

"The LORD detests lying lips, but he delights in people who are trustworthy. Proverbs 12:22"

"I know it well."

"So, here we are, you and me, debating what? But I'll tell you what you should be debating. And that is how to deal with the difference between fact vs. propaganda, coupled with facts vs. lies, and show the millions of Americans in 2024 that there is indeed a difference, and that if too many continue to accept the lies and propaganda of the NEW WORLD ORDER, the DEMOCRATIC PARTY, and the BIDEN AGENDA, that EVIL will win, and everyone, including the mush heads who continued to accept the lies and propaganda of the NEW WORLD ORDER, the DEMOCRATIC PARTY, and the BIDEN AGENDA, will suffer the exact same fate as those who oppose them, meaning the followers of GOOD."

"I want to go back a bit. Why exactly, did God cast you from Heaven?"

"You tell me."

"For the sin of Pride."

"Guilty as charged! And don't forget about the conceit and arrogance that gets added in here and there. Now let me ask you this? Is Pride a form of EVIL, or just a ... tiny sin?"

Chelsea begrudgingly conceded, "Just a sin."

"Exactly!...Meaning that my first sin, and only sin, while in Heaven was not really evil. So, do yourself a big favor and focus on what really matters and that is the NEW WORLD ORDER. And, yes, they are EVIL in its purest form."

Traveler knew that Chelsea had experienced the fury of the NEW WORLD ORDER, both from years of observation and experience to her final experience with her own euthanization at their doing. Nonetheless, Traveler thought it necessary to make her aware of just how long their plans had been in the making.

"Do you understand anything about the NEW WORLD ORDER and their plan for world domination? Do you have any idea when it started, or the tactics and components of their plan, and finally the organizations they utilized to finally get to the GREAT RESET?"

"No, which is why they were able to make it happen."

"True, but in your defense, 99% of the world you are going back to in 2024 don't know either, and that includes the followers and supporters of the NEW WORLD ORDER, the DEMOCRATIC PARTY, and most of the BIDEN ADMINISTRATION. The only difference is that *you* know that the NEW WORLD ORDER is EVIL, and the followers of the NEW WORLD ORDER, the DEMOCRATIC PARTY, and most of the BIDEN ADMINISTRATION are also EVIL by their willingness to voluntarily participate in their plans.

But here is where it gets very complicated. Most followers of GOOD are well aware that the NEW WORLD ORDER, the DEMOCRATIC PARTY, and the BIDEN ADMINISTRATION, through Mass Formation Psychosis and Wrap-up Smear campaigns managed to point the finger and convince their followers that the followers of GOOD were the ones actually guilty of sins, crimes, and evil acts, when they themselves were. That type of mind control is tough to overcome, but it can be done. Are you sure you're up for it?"

"Ready, willing, and anxious."

Though Chelsea was anxious to hear the details, Traveler was going to have to make some tough choices, as telling her everything wouldn't do her much good. Without his intervention or God's direct intervention, Chelsea was up against a stacked-deck in her quest to stop the NEW WORLD ORDER from stealing the 2024 election, and then using it as a stepping stone to total world domination.

Traveler toned down the pace and calmly began his history lesson on the NEW WORLD ORDER.

"The beginnings of the NEW WORLD ORDER started back in the 1700s, in Germany. A group of like-minded, very smart, rich, and affluent men spent months convincing one-another that they, and only they, knew what was best for every person on Earth, meaning in every country and of every religion. They officially formed a pact and called themselves the BAVARIAN ILLUMINATI."

"Okay, stop! I thought that all these stories about the ILLUMINATI were conspiracy theories."

"About that- *Theorizing* that there is a *conspiracy* going on, doesn't mean it's a conspiracy theory. Common sense and logic dictate that once the conspiracy has been proven, it's no longer a theory, but a fact. The term *Conspiracy Theory* is nothing more than a deflective tool of the NEW WORLD ORDER, originally coined by the NEW WORLD ORDER-controlled American CIA, to make everyone readily believe that a story based in fact is merely someone's fantasy, and therefore not to be believed.

But, remember…in 2024, after more than two hundred years of conspiracy theories about the existence of the ILLUMINATI, the modern version, known as the NEW WORLD ORDER suddenly became irrefutable fact when the NEW WORLD ORDER publicly came out of the closet, so to speak, in 2024, and announced their plan for the GREAT RESET. What's interesting about everything I am about to tell you is that it's really not hard to grasp if you can sit back and simply connect the dots. Nothing is ever by accident, or coincidental.

But, even in its infancy, the ILLUMINATI immediately found themselves in direct competition with other world-control groups. Those other groups were the Freemasons and the Roman Catholic Church, with the Roman Catholic Church being controlled by the Jesuits within the highest rankings in the Vatican. For obvious reasons, the Roman Catholic Church wielded the most power and found it easy to ignore the Freemasons, who only wanted to be a cultist and secretive group. On the other hand, the ILLUMINATI scared the Roman Catholic Church, recognizing that the ILLUMINATI didn't want to be a behind-the-scenes group. So, the Roman Catholic Church set out to destroy them, and though the Church silenced them into somewhat obscurity, to try and stay out of the reach of the Church and clandestinely stay viable, the ILLUMINATI went underground, denying they were still active, and began to secretly grow, both in and out of the Roman Catholic Church."

"They actually had agents inside the Catholic Church?"

"Absolutely, including plenty of Cardinals and three Popes. Most are unaware of how powerful the Roman Catholic Church was, and still is, in 2024. Remember, the most powerful families in Europe purposely placed family members into the Church as priests, who then became bishops and archbishops. But the Council of Trent in 1563 was a wake-up call to the families of European royalty, with the Medici family being the biggest example. The Roman Catholic Church separated itself from the families permanently by deciding once and for all that Roman Catholic clergymen could not marry. And the reason for the decision was to insure that upon the death of a clergyman, any money and wealth received by the church would not be shared or passed-on to a surviving widow. It was all about the money and power, and the wealthy families of Europe were just waiting for the opportunity to defect. The Church used the Reformation as a shield to hide the decision at the Council of Trent, much like most of the United States Congress does in passing budget proposals with hidden agendas."

"This is pretty amazing stuff."

"As they say, *seeing is believing*, and I was there to see it. When the ILLUMINATI emerged in the late 1700s it didn't take much to convince the wealthy and powerful families to defect from the Church and join with the ILLUMINATI."

"I never knew any of this."

"As with most things, they did their best to hide it and deny it."

"Wow, I never knew that being dead could have so many perks for a history teacher who basically knew nothing."

Traveler was happy that his understudy was finally starting to grasp it all, and by assimilation would quickly be on-board.

"The ILLUMINATI flexed their muscles a bit in 1795, testing the waters of acceptance by utilizing a modern-day philosopher of the times, named Immanuel Kant, who publicly proposed in his writings, an idea for a *league of nations* to collectively promote peace and control any and all global conflicts. And for the record, Kant was German."

"He started the League of Nations?"

"No, he did not start *The* League of Nations, but merely the idea of "a" league of nations. But now you can see how far back the groundwork was being laid. Are you starting to connect the dots?"

"So far, yes."

"The ILLUMINATI, over the next century was building support and momentum, in part by appealing to and attracting more and more like-minded narcissists with too much money and influence, and looking for a cause. Happily, the ILLUMINATI were able to provide it through inclusion in the group. And then the ILLUMINATI tested their strength and flexed their muscles, by staging WWI."

"Wait. You're saying that the ILLUMINATI started WWI? I thought it was Germany who started it."

"Germany, no. *Germans*, yes. The ILLUMINATI was so devious in their plan that they adopted it as part of their Modus Operandi going forward- Plan something and do something, and convince the world it is somebody else and something else, entirely. The Allies, of which the United States was one, were not fighting Germany. The Allies were fighting the *Central Powers of Europe*. I'm not going to list them for you, but if you were to search who the representatives were and how many individual members there were from all of the Central Powers, your jaw would drop in surprise and disbelief. And what is of interest was that the ILLUMINATI didn't really care which side won the war as WWI was merely a catalyst for their ultimate plan."

"But we won."

"Well, actually, the Central Powers lost, the Allies lost, and the ILLUMINATI won."

"I don't understand."

"Stay with me. Up until WWI the world was a bunch of separate countries with separate governments, separate languages, and separate currencies. The Central Powers brought several countries together, and the Allied forces brought several *other* countries together. Phase I was to gain control of at least 50 independent countries and governments, but the separatism and independence of the countries was the biggest stumbling block for the ILLUMINATI. It's hard to imagine for most mortals that the original members of the ILLUMINATI, who were now *global*, were willing to sacrifice their own countrymen to start and promote WWI. But when you consider that their ultimate goal was to achieve world government unification at the end of the war, the sacrifice of millions, worldwide, in order to stay on track, was of little concern. It was an acceptable means to an end. Maybe you've heard of the term, *collateral damage*.

Surprisingly, it worked, especially because they carefully groomed, and already had, a ready, *willing, and able* pawn, that they helped to get elected - President Woodrow Wilson. Wilson emerged as the most powerful man in the political world, and due to his tappable narcissism believed that he alone was responsible for his ideas and successes, when all the while he was a stooge for the ILLUMINATI."

"Some of this stuff is so hard to believe."

"Which is to their advantage. By the time anyone takes the time to figure it out and expose it, it's too late. Through Wilson, the newly formed LEAGUE OF NATIONS became the impetus to supposedly promote international collective security and free trade. The ILLUMINATI's plans would have been accelerated if it hadn't been for the United States Senate and Congress wishing to tread lightly with Wilson' proposals, meaning that the United States didn't join the very international organization that Wilson proposed. As a result, the United States never officially joined the League of Nations. But behind the scenes there were many rich and powerful individuals and corporations who were loyal to the ILLUMINATI, and were not deterred by the actions of the United States Congress."

"I understand, now, how too much of something can make you want to ignore it."

"Exactly. Now, what other major-control-event over the United States of America also happened under Woodrow Wilson in 1913?"

"I have no idea."

"Again, no one does. Especially the people in 2024. It was the formation of the FEDERAL RESERVE (aka The FED), which was designed to be, and implemented to be the "Central Bank" of the United States. And, whereas the United States Congress kept the United States out of the League of Nations, the ILLUMINATI, via Woodrow Wilson, went right around the Congress and got control of the entire American banking system.

Think about this- When you are going back in 2024, interest rates are at an all-time high. Inflation is at an all-time high. Who controls both of these issues? The FEDERAL RESERVE. I don't need to get into this, and you don't need to talk about it, but one man promised to get to the bottom of the United States banking system's reliance on the FEDERAL RESERVE, which, by the way, *isn't* controlled by the United States Treasury. As a matter of fact, the main purpose of The FED is to *loan* money to the United States, meaning that it also charges the United States interest on the loans to do so.

John Fitgerald Kennedy, better known as JFK, sought to reign in The FED, and declare independence from them. To do so he issued Executive Order 11110 on June 4, 1963, to start the process. Four-and-a-half months later he was assassinated. And with his death was also the death of Executive Order 11110. Who do you think owns and controls The FED?"

Not giving Chelsea a chance to even think about it, Traveler quickly moved on.

"Getting back to World History…ten years after the formation of the LEAGUE OF NATIONS the ILLUMINATI were at it again, believing, that if you don't succeed at first, try again. And it doesn't take much common sense to realize that they *must* have been plotting to make it possible, noting their success in installing a *nothing* Corporal of the German Army in WWI to Chancellor of Germany fifteen years later. You may have heard of him. He was another easily-controlled narcissist, which historically is the main character flaw necessary for exploitation by the ILLUMINATI and NEW WORLD ORDER. His name was Adolph Hitler, who, as the puppet of the ILLUMINATI, plunged the world into WWII. The result was WWII and the death of 50 million people worldwide."

"There is no way I could ever get people to accept these clandestine versions of world history."

"You don't have to and had better not even try. This is strictly for your edification. You just stick with the obvious that is happening in 2024. To continue…

For the second time, the ILLUMINATI, not yet operating as the NEW WORLD ORDER, then proceeded to micro-manage their second United States President, Franklin Delano Roosevelt (FDR). President Franklin Delano Roosevelt resurrected much of what Wilson had started. His Atlantic Charter mirrored much of the principles of Wilson's Fourteen Points plan. And just as the ILLUMINATI had planned, FDR's policies created the International Monetary Fund, the International Bank for Reconstruction and Development, which eventually became the World Bank, and the World Trade Organization - all brainchilds of the ILLUMINATI.

As hoped, the Democrats and Liberals in the United States who had helped to create, promote and approve these organizations foolishly believed that these decisions would benefit the United States of America in a big way. In reality they boosted the weaker countries of the world, giving them an equal voice to the United States in world politics and global economics, thus weakening the United States.

To its credit, there was the Coup de Gras for the ILLUMINATI. It was called THE UNITED NATIONS."

Traveler could see that Chelsea's brain was working overtime to digest all of the facts that he had been throwing at her. Nonetheless, he continued.

"An important note to the UNITED NATIONS is this: When the UNITED NATIONS was formed in 1945, the United States of America had just emerged as the dominant world power at the end of WWII. But the UN CHARTER required *Sovereign Equality* of its members, meaning that The United States was ceding power through the UNITED NATIONS to 49 other nations, many of which were Third World countries. Per the usual, the ILLUMINATI global propaganda machine had everyone convinced this was a great idea, as it would *promote peace and harmony* throughout the world. The UN CHARTER neglected to point out that while the member-countries were holding hands, the ILLUMINATI were arranging for their next global conquest."

"I hate to keep saying it, but I never knew any of this."

"Most don't because it is so complicated that they ignore it. And, as has always been the case, after many years of planning, in 1992, the NEW WORLD ORDER, through the UNITED NATIONS, again tested its influence and power. And I already know that you have never even heard of UN AGENDA 21."

"You're right. I know nothing about any of this. And yes, I'm embarrassed to admit it."

"So much happened right under everyone's eyes, and so much of it went unquestioned and unchallenged. When the UNITED NATIONS AGENDA 2021 was passed in 1992, all 179 of the member nations were completely on-board. But the UNITED NATIONS, meaning the NEW WORLD ORDER, was smart. They didn't immediately start to implement any of it. Once they passed it they just took their time laying the foundations of the plan for a time in the future when they would be in a position to create a global military law situation to seize control of everything.

- *Agenda 21 (Agenda for the 21st Century) is the inventory and control plan for all land, water, minerals, plants, animals, construction, means of production, food, energy, information, education and all human beings in the world.*

It was in fact, the roadmap for global totalitarianism, in conjunction with the NEW WORLD ORDER ideology of "communitarianism," which argues that 'an individual's rights should be balanced against rights of the community.'

Community, however, in the mind of the NEW WORLD ORDER, was made up of nongovernmental organizations (NGOs), corporations, and government, all seemingly independent of one another, but in reality all part of the NEW WORLD ORDER which were to collectively dictate what happened around the world.

The big push for all of this came with the installation of Joe Biden into the Presidency in 2021. Immediately, under the cover of biosecurity and the global COVID-19 pandemic, you saw the emergence of The Green New Deal (Green Agenda), "Build Back

Better," the Fourth Industrial Revolution (the transhumanist movement) and finally, The GREAT RESET finally revealing itself. All of these agendas were in coordination with the General Plan for THE GREAT RESET by the NEW WORLD ORDER.

The *people* were never part of the equation, meaning they would never have a voice in any of the decisions once they had signed-off. It was designed to control every aspect of human existence. And they were successful."

"How many times have I said that I didn't know any of this?"

"It's not like there weren't people out there trying to blow the whistle. There was a book written in 2011 by Rosa Koire, titled, <u>Behind the Green Mask, UN Agenda 21</u>. She said, "Awareness is the first step in Resistance.""

"And?"

"She started out on the right track, debunking the UN's propaganda that the primary goals of Agenda 21 were to *combat environmental damage, poverty, and disease through global cooperation on common interests, mutual needs, and shared responsibilitie*s. But, from her own experience and investigations, she pointed out that Agenda 21 was simply a blueprint for the goal of controlling both national and local governments."

"So, when you hear UNITED NATIONS, just know that we're talking about the NEW WORLD ORDER?"

"Plain and simple."

"How successful was she in exposing them?"

"Moderately, but her biggest mistake was believing, as a Democrat, that exposing UNITED NATIONS AGENDA 21 would be something that the Democratic National Committee and all Democrats would embrace. If she only knew...."

"Is she still alive when I go back?"

"No. She died in 2021. But even if she were still alive it wouldn't matter because in 2024 the NEW WORLD ORDER and all of its member-collaborators aren't hiding anymore. They don't have to hide, because the opposition is a bunch of....Let me take a different approach, and helping you to understand that you aren't just fighting the forces of EVIL.

You will also be fighting the forces of GOOD, mainly Republicans, who are too caught up in their own egos and narcissism to want to do anything but puff their chests out and get reelected to Congress."

"Oh, my... It sounds like you're actually showing signs of human frustration and anger."

"I'm way beyond that, because if you're not successful and EVIL wins the 2024 election, I am looking at the groveling you alluded to."

"Not even I want that, if it means losing mankind."

"Ever since the second bite-and-snap of the apple, I knew Man was in trouble."

"Second bite?"

"Hellooo...I took the first bite, and Eve took the second bite. It was then I knew that Mankind was in trouble. And because of it, if I were human, I'm pretty sure I'd be leaning toward misogyny."

"After your comment about Eve, I'm not surprised."

"Well, if you think about it, Eve was the only woman on Earth. It was one thing for me to tempt her, but it was a whole other thing for her to tempt Adam. Mine was to prove it could be done. In her case, there was an ulterior motive. See the difference?"

"I'm thinking."

"Times up! But there is very good news for when you go back, and I encourage you to do this. If you can get the support of the Republican *women* in Congress, you're going to be much better off. The women will be a support vehicle for you because they are the only ones who know what the shortest distance is between two dots.

Too many of the men are namby-pamby wusses, who spend more time *hemming and hawing* than they do solving problems. And it is the sole reason why the NEW WORLD ORDER was able to steal the 2024 election."

"What is namby-pamby?"

"Look it up. Without true leadership, all that is GOOD will simply fade away, and quite quickly. Leadership is the main driving force for motivation. Without motivation, Republicans, Conservatives, and reborn Democrats will stay home on election day. And if they do, you will have wasted your time in going back."

"I'm a little surprised that a bigger effort wasn't made to stop all of this."

"It has a lot to do with the sucker mentality of Americans, starting at the highest levels of government. For starters, the Republicans were the real morons, by doing what they always had done. They let the dictates of the NEW WORLD ORDER and the DEMOCRATIC PARTY run rampant over the United States, and the world for that matter, through the UNITED NATIONS. The Republicans talked a big story, but rarely acted on it. And not surprisingly, the NEW WORLD ORDER acted repeatedly and successfully. But I can tell you with certainty, that if Donald Trump had won in 2020, the United States would *not* have stayed a member of the UNITED NATIONS for very long. And the NEW WORLD ORDER knew it, which is why he had to go."

"You think Donald Trump would have pulled us out of the United Nations?"

"And NATO. He would have had no choice, as the UN AGENDA 21/30 required total capitulation of the United States to the UNITED NATIONS and NEW WORLD ORDER, and Donald Trump would have never let it happen."

"It sure would have been a different and much better world, had Trump stayed in office."

"Well, hopefully your efforts will give him a second chance. Keep in mind that AGENDA 21 will be in a circling pattern, so to speak, when you get back to 2024. The bigger and final push will be the Pandemic of 2029, and as a result, the simultaneous implementation of UNITED NATIONS 2030 Agenda and the BIG RESET."

"Is the 2030 version any different from the 2021 version?"

"It gets more into catering to Leftist ideologies, to garner support, but the ultimate goal is the same. Their own website read:

The Global Goals and the 2030 Agenda for Sustainable Development seek to end poverty and hunger, realize the human rights of all, achieve gender equality and the empowerment of all women and girls, and ensure the lasting protection of the planet and its natural resources. The Global Goals are integrated and indivisible, and balance the three dimensions of sustainable development: the economic, social and environmental.

Now take a closer look at the 17 Sustainable Development Goals (SDGs) from this Agenda, and then ask yourself: *Why would any American want a globalist organization, with its own agendas, dictating to the United States how it should be running this country?*"

"Which is why our only hope is going to be Donald Trump."

"From your lips to God's ears…One, last, very important thought- Think about how the 2030 Agenda of the UNITED NATIONS coincides, by time and messaging with the GREAT RESET of 2030, as outlined by Klaus Schwab's WORLD ECONOMIC FORUM. It was two, *seemingly* separate *world* organizations proposing the exact same thing. And every country in the world, through a single representative, went along with it."

"How come the WORLD ECONOMIC FORUM lived on after he died?"

"Biblically speaking, because the Seven-headed Dragon still had six heads left."

"This is when I wished I weren't dead, so I could cry. How could we have been so stupid, and blind?"

"Well, it's time to get everyone to open their eyes, and keep them open. Remember, the Year 2024 was a major turning point for the NEW WORLD ORDER and the DEMOCRATIC PARTY. The success of the COVID pandemic had proven that the United States of America, the largest domino in the free world, was extremely vulnerable to every part of the NEW WORLD ORDER and DEMOCRATIC PARTY's devastating plot to overturn the United States government, seize control of the military, and bring the masses into total submission to the NEW WORLD ORDER, knowing that, *as goes the United States of America, so goes the entire world.*

Keeping a NEW WORLD ORDER pawn in the White House in the 2024 election was critical to their plan."

"Until the 2024 WORLD ECONOMIC FORUM in Davos, Switzerland, most residents of planet Earth were ignorant and clueless about the existence of the NEW WORLD ORDER, until it publicly and boldly admitted to its existence, by name, as the NEW WORLD ORDER. They also made clear, their One-World vision. Up until that time they had been denying their existence as the ILLUMINATI, but were now ready to publicly emerge as the NEW WORLD ORDER and let the minions of their messaging, namely MSN, MSNBC, and Social Media, be the deflectors and dissuaders of their subversive agenda and well-guarded plan to rule the world.

But, in true ignorance of the admissions before them, the peoples and governments of the world *yawned*, and let the NEW WORLD ORDER, the DEMOCRATIC PARTY, the UNITED NATIONS, and the WORLD HEALTH ORGANIZATION put their plan for world domination into an out-in-the-open pathway. George Orwell was rolling over in his grave.

Not only had they uncloaked their very existence as the NEW WORLD ORDER, but doubled-down at the WORLD ECONOMIC FORUM unveiling THE GREAT RESET, which was dependent on the selfishness and shallowness of Liberals who only needed a single item of concern to keep them loyal to the cause. And years of the in-your-face issues of Climate Change, fossil fuels, ALPHABET rights, transgender athlete rights, feminist rights, abortion rights, speech suppression, anti-family values, anti-religious values, BLM, ANTIFA, Critical Race Theory, and Defund the Police initiatives, were nothing more that smoke and mirrors to deflect from the real agenda.

The World Economic Forum had made their goals clear, actually publishing on its website a list of "predictions" for 2030, that was scrubbed and re-written, of course.

1. You'll own nothing and be happy.
2. The United States won't be the world's superpower.
3. You won't die waiting for an organ donor.
4. You'll eat less meat.
5. A billion people will be displaced by climate change.
6. You could be preparing to go to Mars.
7. Western values will be tested to their breaking point.
8. Fossil fuels will be eliminated.

Whereas they provided eight (8) promises, in truth there were only three (3) that were part of their grand scheme. Number 1 was a given. Number 2 was a necessity. Number 5 was a typical NEW

WORLD ORDER practice of telling half-truths, meaning that two billion people would be displaced, keeping in mind that the Climate Change they were really talking about was the one-thousand-degree temperature inside the crematoriums where they planned to reduce the bodies of the two billion, to ashes, so they could easily dispose of them.

And as history bore out in real time, starting with the Pandemic of 2029, every one of the eight promises came true, with a few surprises thrown in for good measure."

Looking back, Chelsea, didn't feel any better about not recognizing all that was clearly in front of her and most of the world. She was beginning to question her fortitude to carry out that which was the only option for the human race to get a second chance. "What do you think my chances are?"

"It might be easier than you think. You're not going to be singlehandedly fighting a war against the physical oppression of the NEW WORLD ORDER. That particular war already cost you your life. But in 2024 the NEW WORLD ORDER doesn't have total control yet. It was and will be all about the presidential election. If the DEMOCRATIC PARTY manages to stay in power, meaning the NEW WORLD ORDER staying in power, you will experience Déjà vu all over again."

"That means I will know what is going to happen and will have to suffer through it until they euthanize me, a second time?"

"It's the price you'll pay for going back."

"That's asking quite a lot of me."

"It's your choice. But, you are the only hope at this point. I cannot stress enough what must be the driving force behind your quest:

When GOOD wins, everybody wins, including the followers of EVIL. It has always been that way. But when EVIL wins, everybody loses."

"I guess I will never understand how anyone could ever think that winning, meaning destroying humanity as a whole, could be a justification for their actions."

"And you've never been alone in that. But it was also by choice that the primary target was the United States of America, because Americans have traditionally suffered from two forms of vulnerability. The first has always been vanity. Americans, since the first day of the Republic, at the end of the Revolutionary War, have believed that America was invincible. Granted it proved the brag over and over through countless wars but war with the NEW WORLD ORDER was not a shooting war. It was a war of words and wills. The NEW WORLD ORDER had the will to succeed, and America as a whole, didn't have the will to fight them until it was too late."

"You're right. But you said there were two."

"The second vulnerability was that Americans were raised to be too nice, too honorable, too accommodating, too..."

"Okay, I get it. As you already said, we were just suckers waiting to be taken."

"Congratulations. You're finally getting it."

"I have a question that seems to be a missing component of all of this. What was the reward for all of the followers of the NEW WORLD ORDER?

"On the short-term, money. Do you have any idea how much money was thrown at NEW WORLD ORDER-loving companies in the United States alone? Trillions."

"Trillions?"

"Did anyone think that the US debt, under BIDEN, climbed another SIX TRILLION DOLLARS because of COVID or bad management? No, it grew because the NEW WORLD ORDER was making sure that multi-billions got doled out to a lot of entities, here and there, over several years. And it started with Obama and his

NEW WORLD ORDER Green Energy agenda in which companies were formed, subsidized by the government, and then disappeared over night. Did anyone think to ask where the billions actually went? Remember – by controlling enough you will eventually control all.

And money was the bait to accomplish it. From there the NEW WORLD ORDER, the DEMOCRATIC PARTY, and the JOE BIDEN ADMINISTRATION used the bought-and-paid-for companies to help gain the CONTROL over enough to accomplish their goals. To remind you, EVIL was quite successful in the year 2024 in convincing far too many that the One-World, One-People vision of the future was somehow utopian. And too many bought into the propaganda, lies, and indoctrination.

What you have to recognize, going all the way back to the beginnings of the ILLUMINATI is that they were very smart, devious, and determined individuals, who, working collectively, were extremely successful. Think about this- They gave trillions to people to basically buy them off into being followers, and at the same time, through their years of propaganda, lies, and indoctrination, convinced the very same people that they had no worth; that the only way for them to have worth was to destroy those who actually had worth, meaning people who enjoyed freedom, people of faith, and people with close family ties, until such time as no one had anything, meaning that then, and only then, would everyone be equal. All of it was in keeping with the first promise of the Great Reset - *You'll own nothing and be happy*. And that is what you will be up against."

"I don't know if I can do this. I'm scared."

"Of knowing what you're up against or what the outcome of failure will be?"

"More about the failure aspect. It's almost as if I will be responsible for it happening if I cannot stop it."

"This knowledge you have gained should not be a deterrent. It should be your rallying cry. You saw for yourself the world in 2036. EVIL had won, and the biggest losers were the followers of EVIL who suddenly realized that the NEW WORLD ORDER only needed them until they didn't need them anymore; meaning, once the goal had been achieved, the minions become expendable. And that's who you have to get to. The followers of GOOD won't need convincing, but the followers of EVIL will."

"How can I do that?"

"Through personal strength, endurance, determination, and the sincere belief that you *can* do it. In the Year 2024, when you want to go back there is no disputing that MASS FORMATION PSYCHOSIS is in full force and effect by the NEW WORLD ORDER, the JOE BIDEN ADMINISTRATION, and the DEMOCRATIC PARTY. If you are able to even get a small number of the followers of EVIL to get on board, you're all set. There is definitely strength in numbers."

"Okay, stop. Backup. What is Mass Formation Psychosis?"

"In the war of GOOD vs. EVIL, *EVIL* will always win in the end because GOOD thinks the best way to win an argument, a fight, a battle, or a war, is to play nice. When has EVIL ever played nice? And the problem with *playing nice* is that peoples of most religions, and especially Born-Again Christians who are so reliant on Biblical teachings and prophesies for example, are always willing to accept defeat, rationalizing it with everything from turning the other cheek to, "Oh, we'll get our revenge when the Rapture comes."

"What's wrong with that?"

"Hey, if that's what you believe, and what you think the final answer is, then why bother going back?"

"I accept what the Bible teaches. It says..."

"Says what? Maybe at some point you should start paying attention to what it really says, not what you've been told it says. It says, allowing me to paraphrase and combine the hundreds of versions that I know of, '...*that believers will be resurrected and joined with Christians who are still alive on Earth, to meet the Lord...,*' *etcetera, etcetera.*"

Chelsea is trying to find the words to ask what he is trying to convey.

"Again, I am not trying to question or condemn any part of your faith, whatsoever. But you have to look at the facts as you know them. For starters, why do people who have already earned Heaven need to be resurrected? They're already there. They've already been *raptured*. Secondly, and FYI, by 2038 there won't be anyone left to rapture. So, just go back to Heaven, let the NEW WORLD ORDER have its way, and when the Rapture comes, you can ask for permission to personally greet *no one*, because the NEW WORLD ORDER is going to wipe out anyone who even thinks about God, Heaven, Religion, the Rapture, or anything else."

"I can't accept that there won't be a Rapture."

"Then go back and make sure that EVIL is vanquished, GOOD wins, and there are millions left to be raptured when the time comes."

Chelsea was consumed in thought, realizing that everything Traveler had said was seemingly true.

"I accept what you have said, and I also accept the challenge to stop EVIL from winning. I am determined more than ever to go back and stop them."

"Amen. Now, what else do you want to know?"

"I need to have a better understanding as to how they were so successful in corrupting so many."

"How they were so successful was that they were effective in utilizing simultaneous ploys that fed on one-another. Think about the Freemasons and the "seeing eye" at the top of the pyramid on the American dollar bill. The "eye" sees that everything is reduced to three things, and each one feeds and supports the others. The "eye" sees that the three points of the pyramid are money, information, and influence, with each of those three having subcategories. The Freemasons learned centuries ago that money begets information and influence; information begets influence and money; influence begets money and information. If you control one, you eventually control all. From their continued successes the NEW WORLD ORDER was able to take the concept to a new level.

Obviously, they mastered the pyramid, but they also figured out, and implemented a plan by which the main pyramid can also be the top of a much bigger pyramid. Think of it as a pyramid scheme on steroids, as was a familiar description of many things in your lifetime.

But here is the biggest problem that you are going to have in your re-do, and the answer to your question. You are dealing with something much more powerful and sinister than simply a war of words. You will be challenged everyday by *Mass Formation Psychosis*. Going all the way back to 1895, a French psychologist named Gustav Le Bon wrote *The Crowd: A Study of the Popular Mind*. He theorized that a crowd develops a psychology of its own that seizes the minds of each individual in the crowd; that the psychology of a *crowd* is impulsive, irrational, and resistant to reason. In modern times the crowd became easily manipulated, using one of its greatest successes as the catalyst for the manipulation. Nancy Pelosi, herself, uncloaked its use and named it: *Wrap-up Smear campaigns*. To make it easier to understand, at its core it follows the old adage that, *You can't un-ring a bell.*

In modern times, meaning the times of the NEW WORLD ORDER, the *crowd*, utilizing Mass Formation Psychosis, became more violent, which was inevitable because they were being fueled by Wrap-up Smear campaigns and then, the *crowd*, as you knew it, became a MOB, making the NEW WORLD ORDER more successful as the NEW WORLD ORDER is basically a synonym for MOB RULE. And if history has taught you anything, its first lesson is that a MOB is always evil. And the second lesson is that a MOB is never right."

"To better understand this, is there one, specific example of this to put it into perspective?"

"The best example, especially in the year 2024 would be *Trump Derangement Syndrome*. The Syndrome has all of the elements in play to keep the followers of the NEW WORLD ORDER, the DEMOCRATIC PARTY, and BIDEN SUPPORTERS in line, and receptive to the continued onslaught of lies, propaganda, and indoctrination that the NEW WORLD ORDER outlets regularly spewed. Trump was not only the NEW WORLD ORDER's common target, meaning their unifying target, just as the unfounded hatred of Jews was to Hitler's Third Reich messaging. Oddly, and I know this, most of the people suffering from it know they are suffering from it, and oddly are proud to be suffering from it. Yet, if asked one direct question, which is, *Why exactly do you hate Donald Trump?,* they can't give you a definitive answer. The most common answer will be, after great hesitation, "... Well.... because... he's Donald Trump."

"I remember experiencing that myself. They ignored the Donald Trump who made the country the best it had ever been, and focused on a bunch of lies and propaganda. But, you have to admit, in some ways he brought it on himself."

"I don't agree with that, but for the sake of argument, I'll hear you out."

"I'm talking about that time on the bus when he made some lewd comments."

"You're talking about the incident in 2005 when he was doing a segment with Billy Bush."

"Exactly. And he said what he had done to women, which even as a Trump supporter, it was hard to defend."

"What that was, was a prime example of a Wrap-up Smear."

"How is that a Wrap-up Smear? As Pelosi herself, said, A Wrap-up Smear is when you deliberately tell a lie about someone, and then feed it to the press and let them run with it to ruin someone."

"Exactly."

"But Trump said it."

"Said what?"

"That he had grabbed a woman's...privates."

"Actually, he didn't."

"Of course he did. I heard it myself, more than once."

"Oh, you heard it, for sure, but you didn't *listen* to what he actually said, meaning that you, as was every other American, were *told* what you heard by the NEW WORLD ORDER and the DEMOCRATIC PARTY. And, as was the intent, Americans simply accepted what *they* wanted you to *think* he said."

"All right, what is going on here? Are you trying to tell me that Donald Trump never said that he grabbed women... you know where?"

"That's exactly what I'm saying."

"But I heard him."

"No, you didn't. What Donald Trump said, was, ...'And when you're a star they let you do it.' Now, *that* statement specifically referred to kissing them- nothing else. Then he continued with the part that the Wrap-up Smear focused on, '…You can do anything. Grab them by the (privates). You can do anything.' Okay. Now that you know what to listen for, listen to it in his own words."

Traveler magically brought up the 2005 video of the incident for Chelsea to watch. When it was over he immediately played it for her again. Chelsea's was showing signs of amazement as Trump's words were played out.

"So tell me. Did Donald Trump ever say that he had done it? To anyone? Ever? No. He never said that *he* actually did anything."

Chelsea was almost embarrassed that she had fallen for the NEW WORLD ORDER and DEMOCRATIC PARTY Wrap-up Smear about the incident.

"You're right. He said one thing, and then the Media Sites simply told us that he said something else, and we all bought it."

"Hook, line, and sinker, as the saying goes. You see, Trump was doing exactly what he said he was doing. It was slangily called *locker talk*. Men did it all the time. They brag about things they have done and never did, could do but never would, and would never do, even if given the chance. And it actually gets funnier as it gets told over and over because the claims get more outlandish with every telling. But the NEW WORLD ORDER and the DEMOCRATIC PARTY seized the opportunity to tell everyone what he had said, even though they knew that it wasn't what he had said at all. And that, was the Wrap-up Smear."

"That's amazing."

"Now that I have explained how MASS FORMATION PSYCHOSIS is the NEW WORLD ORDER'S and DEMOCRATIC PARTY'S greatest tool, let me give you one more example of how they used it in 2024, when you will be going back. I'm specifically referring to how the NEW WORLD ORDER- controlled Media Sites used the Wrap-up Smear and Mass Formation Psychosis to create the narrative that Donald Trump would be a dictator, which in truth was a clever ploy to deflect from the actions of the real dictator, Joe Biden."

"When you see corruption being rewarded and honesty becoming a self-sacrifice - You may know that your society is doomed."
Ayn Rand, Atlas Shrugged, 1957

"Sometimes, even the smartest of politicians can unknowingly walk into a hornet's nest. Donald Trump did it when he said he was going to be a *One-Day Dictator*, immediately trying to clarify it to say that he would immediately, by Executive Order, order the drilling for oil by the United States to start the process to again achieve Energy Independence. And in true NEW WORLD ORDER, DEMOCRATIC PARTY, and ALL MEDIA SITES controlled by the NEW WORLD ORDER fashion, they fed the psychosis of their already brainwashed minions to push the narrative that Donald Trump would be a *real* dictator; that somehow he was going to seize absolute power over the federal government.

How conveniently they wanted to divert the attention from what a Real Dictator actually looks like, meaning JOE BIDEN. Here is what Joe Biden did-

- In his first month in office he revoked 32% of Trump's actions, including the Keystone XL pipeline, and stopped the building of the wall between the USA and Mexico.

- He abandoned Title IX protections for biological women in favor of anyone who wanted to play female sports that wasn't a biological woman.

- In his first 9 days in office, he ordered 59 Executive Actions.

- In his first 3 ½ years in office he demanded 138 Executive Orders, 607 Proclamations, 173 Memoranda, 121 Notices, and 42 Determinations.

- In 2024 BIDEN proclaimed that Easter Sunday will be *Trans Visibility Day.*

- In true dictatorial fashion he ignored a ruling by the US Supreme Court that he didn't have the authority to cancel student loan debt, and then publicly thumbed his nose at the Supreme Court and all Americans by ordering it anyway. (Keep in mind that even Nancy Pelosi publicly announced that he didn't have the authority to cancel student debt.)

- Cancelled the college loans debts totaling $1.4 TRILLION DOLLARS, which taxpayers would have to pay.

- Opened US borders to anyone and everyone who wanted to enter, illegally, and granted them amnesty once they managed to set foot on American soil. Though the actual number will never be known by anyone in 2024, the BIDEN ADMINISTRATION floated a number of over 7 million illegal entries through June 2024, since he took office. Knowing the BIDEN ADMINISTRATION, it means it was closer to 12 million. Did you know that in 2005, according to the US Government Committee on Government Reform, there were already between 10-12 million illegal immigrants in the United States?

- Under JOE BIDEN, ONE TRILLION DOLLARS was spent on illegal subsidies by the end of 2024. It also meant that hundreds of people on the TERRORIST WATCH LIST entered the country. It also meant that another 200,000+ convicted felons had entered the country. It also meant that the NEW WORLD ORDER, the DEMOCRATIC PARTY, and the BIDEN ADMINISTRATION didn't care what anyone thought. Just vote for them, and Shut Up!

- Rolled back all Trump-era sanctions against Iran, which meant another 90 Billion Dollars for Iran to support terrorism in the Middle East. All of the money that Iran suddenly made under BIDEN went to terrorist groups, like HAMAS, who used the money to fund the war against Israel.

- Froze all domestic oil production, which meant Iran made another 35 Billion dollars in three years from America buying their oil.

- Rolled back all sanctions and let them continue to build nuclear bombs, which Iran had vowed to use against Israel first, and the United States shortly thereafter.

- Supported HAMAS and withheld the weapons, approved by Congress, needed for Israel to fight HAMAS.

This, easily verifiable evidence of JOE BIDEN, with the support of the NEW WORLD ORDER and the DEMOCRATIC PARTY, is glaring proof of what an American President Dictator actually looks like. But as the NEW WORLD ORDER proved over and over, Americans will just sit back and let it happen."

"Though it may not appear to be so, the NEW WORLD ORDER, with the support of the DEMOCRATIC PARY and most MEDIA SITES, is a textbook definition of Mob Rule. And in case you're curious what the accepted definition of Mob Rule actually is, seeing as no one has access anymore to most dictionaries or books of any historical or educational value, it is defined as, *control of political situations outside of the conventional and/or legal realm. And, it typically involves violence and intimidation.*

Could anyone ever come up with a better definition of the NEW WORLD ORDER, the DEMOCRATIC PARTY, and the JOE BIDEN ADMINISTRATION playbook from 2020 onward, when Joe Biden became President? The NEW WORLD ORDER, DEMOCRATIC PARTY, and JOE BIDEN propaganda machine fueled the hysteria, using all of the tools in their arsenal, including Mass Formation Psychosis and Pelosi's Wrap-up Smear. These fueled the MOB mentality, and we now know what the result was.

Part of the process the NEW WORLD ORDER and DEMOCRATIC PARTY figured out was that the best way to suppress the answers is to suppress the questions. Eventually, if enough stop thinking and asking questions, they surrender their free will, and logic no longer becomes necessary. The acceptors of this become the Mob, and when Mob Rule becomes the law of the land, you end up where you were in 2036. Therefore, Censorship is another one of their biggest weapons.

Also remember that when you and half of the world were not paying attention in the 2020s, there was a world-renowned doctor, biochemist, and infectious disease researcher named Robert Malone, who actually helped to develop the mRNA vaccine technology. Yet, when he came out against that technology being used for Covid vaccines, the entire NEW WORLD ORDER machine turned on him and made it their mission to discredit him. And what did the rest of the NEW WORLD ORDER MOB do, in keeping with the NEW WORLD ORDER's Mass Formation Psychosis? They blindly joined-in to the hysteria to make it so the messaging stayed in full force and effect, ensuring that the money train would continue to roll for those at the top of the food chain. And part of that was the Covid vaccination. The vaccine was their communion."

"Why did you call the vaccine, communion?"

"That, came from a man named Jason Whitlock, in and of the times that you will be back on Earth. He said that the NEW WORLD ORDER types, '...condemn religion, especially Christianity, yet adhere to one of its most revered practice; that of Holy Communion...their communion is the Covid vaccine.' He was a smart man. And a good man. I hope you run into him."

"Was?"

"Let's just say that in 2024, he's around and willing to talk."

"Boy, the NEW WORLD ORDER sure pulled a fast one on the world by making the vaccination mandatory."

"You still had a choice, at that time."

"No I didn't. I was a teacher and my mission in life was to be around to help people, and I couldn't do that if I had refused the vaccination."

"You still had a choice. You did it, and then they fired you anyway. But how many did you know who did it because they were so taken by the government propaganda machine, promoting a campaign that it was the end of the world if you didn't take it; that you were endangering yourself, your family, your friends and co-workers, and the world, if you didn't do it?"

"I had some co-workers who were absolutely psycho about it."

"And "psycho," is by definition, suffering from a psychosis. Getting the picture? That, in and unto itself should have been the wake-up call, but the governments of the world who were in bed with the NEW WORLD ORDER already, via the UNITED NATIONS and the WORLD HEALTH ORGANIZATION, were willing to use their positions to force the masses into doing it. And, the "how" comes right back to MASS FORMATION PSYCHOSIS and MOB RULE. Got it?"

"Got it."

"It's an ingenious way of doing things. You start out with a plan, get 1% on board, who get another 10% on board, and by the time you get to 30% on board, you have enough in the right places, to control the masses. And in the case of Covid, the world."

"It's hard to believe that 30% can control the other 70 %."

Traveler continued to unveil historical facts that most never paid attention to.

"When Hitler took power in the 1930s, and then catapulted Germany into WWII against the entire free world, how many citizens of Germany do you think were actually members of the Nazi Party?"

"Most of them?"

"See, even *that* propaganda worked."

"What propaganda?"

"That it takes as many as 30% to control the other 70%. It's a way for the NEW WORLD ORDER, in this case, to say that it's impossible for so few to control so many, all the while knowing that it had already been proven that much less is necessary to be successful, and it resulted in World War II."

"So, how many?"

"5% before the war started. Toward the end of the war, in 1945, about 10%."

"How could 95% of the citizens of Germany allow a nut-case like Hitler to do that to them?"

"Because the ILLUMINATI, through Hitler, knew that if they could control the most important 5%, which meant the entire military, it would ensure complete power. But to get everyone else on board you need a common enemy. Point the finger at what you want everyone to believe is the cause of all of the problems and let the government propaganda machine fuel the Mass Formation Psychosis. In this case, the NEW WORLD ORDER chose the Jews in Germany to be the common enemy, and Hitler enforced it. Actually they were an easy target because in 1933, Jews in Germany were only three-quarters of a percent (.075%) of the total population, numbering a little over 500,000. The Jews, themselves, were no threat to Hitler or his war machine. They were doctors, lawyers, engineers, and shop keepers. But that also meant that they were well-educated, and anyone trying to seize power simply cannot have educated people questioning their actions or motives."

"And in 2021, the common enemy was Covid 19?"

"Yes. Successfully, they shifted the Mass Formation Psychosis from people to a man-made pandemic. What's interesting about the Mass Formation Psychosis of the COVID pandemic was that they were able to scare the world into believing their lies and propaganda, again by having only 5% on board. "

"What 5%?"

"The NEW WORLD ORDER already controlled the WORLD HEALTH ORGANIZATION, which in turn controlled the AMERICAN MEDICAL ASSOCIATION (AMA), which controlled every doctor in the country. It was easy. And there is your 5%. Interestingly, there were plenty of doctors around the world trying to put the brakes on, with regard to protocols and taking a *not-so-fast* approach to the vaccination plans. So, as expected, the NEW WORLD ORDER, the WHO, the CDC, BIG

PHARMA, and the BIDEN ADMINISTRATION set out to silence the dissenters, and got all of SOCIAL MEDIA on board to help. Now, it was all about Censorship."

"It's amazing that there are so many examples of what they got away with."

"It was a self-propagating success story. The COVID test-run of 2020 and the world decimating Pandemic of 2029, which was a strain of COVID on steroids. But the key to getting people on board with the vaccine in 2029 was to show proof of how *good* the vaccine-science had gotten, by pointing to the vaccine that had immediately wiped out another man-made pathogen- the Bird Flu in 2026.

THE NEW WORLD ORDER needed the Bird Flu pandemic in 2026 to reaffirm to the world that their vaccines were effective, and prove to themselves that they could control the narrative to their absolute advantage. They created the Bird Flu and the *cure*, in a vaccine, simultaneously. It had to be about vaccines, and nothing else.

At the infancy stages of the COVID outbreak in 2020 there were a few different drugs that many doctors were prescribing, and with very good results. But the NEW WORLD ORDER and BIG PHARMA, in collusion with the WORLD HEALTH ORGANIZATION, the CDC, and the AMA couldn't allow that to happen. So, in a *true* conspiracy, they shut down the availability of the prescriptions, which most of the larger drug store chains got on board with, and pounded-home the messaging, also known as lies, propaganda and indoctrination, that the vaccine, which was forthcoming, was the *only* answer to stopping and curing the virus. In the meantime, 80% of the people worldwide, who died of Covid 19 died because of being denied access to the prescription pills that would have cured them in three days. Conversely, the colluders also prescribed protocols that caused deaths, like ventilators. Both of these scenarios paved the way for an unproven vaccine, which was never a vaccine under the laws at the time, to be the only acceptable course of action."

"I remember the ventilator debacle. Many of us were wondering how much money was made by all of those ventilators."

"Billions! Remember! *Nine* billionaires were created in less than a year amongst the BIG PHARMA ranks, because of the so-called vaccines. What is interesting is that all of these people thought they were getting more powerful, more important, and therefore less expendable, by being richer. In the end it didn't save any of them-not from the NEW WORLD ORDER, and more importantly, not from God."

"I'm on board with that one - To *HELL* with them!"

"Also remember that I'm the Greeter. Definitely a perk when it comes to seeing the shocked looks on their EVIL faces when they say, 'What? Hell is real?' The NEW WORLD ORDER lied to me?'

Here's another example, and closer to the time you're going back. Do you remember back in 2023 and 2024 when the NEW WORLD ORDER, the DEMOCRATIC PARTY, the WORLD HEALTH ORGANIZATION, BIG PHARMA, and the CDC were pushing the idea of *Long Covid?*"

"I remember something about it, but I'm not sure what it really meant."

"What it meant was that it was an excuse to continue to get Covid boosters, and to continue forcing people to self-test. It was amazing to me that no one questioned what BIG PHARMA did with the millions of self-test kits that had expired."

"What did they do?"

"They simply put stickers on the boxes that extended the expiration dates."

"They had expired?"

"Absolutely. The problem was that most of the world began to accept that the dangers of Covid were over, so people stopped using them. In order to keep the money rolling in and continually fuel more fear, they created a *Wrap-Up* type of narrative that everyone had to be concerned with *Long COVID*, meaning that the masses had to continue to test, and also that they needed more and more boosters. They just sat back and let the PSYCHOIS take it from there. It was by design to get as many as possible to accept that vaccines were the answer to everything."

"One last thought. In June 2024, when you are going back, a two-and-a-half-year study that was done by Ohio State University researchers determined from *statistical data,* that the COVID-19 patients who had been vaccinated and then hospitalized after coming down with the disease had a significantly higher mortality rate than *unvaccinated* patients who had also been hospitalized. And the NEW WORLD ORDER, predictably did everything in its power to bury the reporting."

"Based on *statistical data*?"

"Absolutely. It was also determined that age and comorbidities played no role in the statistics. To take it a step further, when you go back, pay attention to the Defender, an online goldmine of information on COVID. They also reported in June 2024 that studies were coming in from all over the world showing that there were over Three Million *excess* deaths from Covid, worldwide, meaning the protocols that BIG PHARMA, the WHO, and most governments forced on the people, and specifically the mRNA Covid vaccine, were contributory to the deaths. That's based only on the information that was available. Imagine what the NEW WORLD ORDER, BIG PHARMA, and the WHO were able to suppress.

Before the ink was dry on that report, another report emerged that was done by Oxford University, describing how cases of myocarditis and pericarditis had been soaring in kids under 15 since the rollout of COVID vaccine shots in 2021. The report was released to call out the lies of TONY FAUCI, the CDC, BIG PHARMA, the WHO, and many international government agencies controlled by the NEW WORLD ORDER, who lied about the necessity of having children vaccinated.

The conclusions from the Oxford University report, based on the study of One Million children in the UK, between the ages of 5 and 15 were:

- One of the biggest *scare tactics* used by NEW WORLD ORDER minions, including BIG PHARMA, the WHO, the CDC, and many international government agencies was, *if children did NOT get vaccinated, then the risk of myocarditis from COVID was a great possibility.*
- Not one, single, *unvaccinated* child in the study developed myocarditis, pericarditis, or any other form of heart failure during the term of the study (2021-2023)
- ALL of the *unvaccinated* children who contracted COVID easily recovered from it.
- **100% of all of the children who actually developed heart conditions, were vaccinated.**

But there is more confirmation of how vaccines are the propaganda arm of the NEW WORLD ORDER. In California, in June 2024, there was something going on in pediatrics that was illegal at the least and unethical on a grand scale. I'm referring to the fact that more than one-half of all pediatricians were refusing to take on new patients, meaning babies, if the parents were not going to follow the CDC guidelines for vaccinations."

"How did they get away with that?"

"Who was going to enforce the law? The Biden Administration? The Newsom Administration? The CDC? The WHO? BIG PHARMA? It certainly wasn't going to be the California Stoogeon General."

"I obviously wasn't a parent so I knew nothing about this."

"It wasn't that complicated. The CDC guidelines for newborns required 7 vaccinations at two months of age. Then repeat the 7 vaccinations at four months of age. To complete the cycle, the CDC requirement was to repeat the 7 vaccinations.   Then they wanted babies to get a batch of 7*different* vaccinations at twelve months of age.   At fifteen months the requirement was 4 more *different* vaccinations, to include the COVID vaccination, in spite of all studies that showed how dangerous and unnecessary it was for children."

"And no one was able to stop them."

"No one tried. The plan was to force parents to submit, or lose medical care for their children. Most did it, some didn't. But again, vaccinations was their communion, and they wanted to force the masses onto their knees and do what they were told. "

"They were nothing but slimes... Am I allowed to say that?"

"With my blessing. But in the end, the doctors who were part of this, were not too happy to see me."

"Omission is the most powerful form of lie."   *- George Orwell*

"Censorship, at its core, is lying. Not telling people the truth, and simultaneously not allowing anyone else to tell the truth, through Censorship, is tantamount to lying, pure and simple. What the NEW WORLD ORDER Media Outlets also believe is, *they are telling you the truth if you don't know it's a lie.*

Surprisingly, even the EVIL have a moment of clarity, as shown by a former leftist President.

"The road to tyranny, we must never forget, begins with the destruction of the truth."   *-Bill Clinton*

The irony of Bill Clinton's statement lies in the fact that he was married to the most prolific liar and most corrupt politician in the history of American politics. Hillary Clinton saw the truth in the statement and did everything possible to make sure that destruction of the truth was her primary goal."

"I thought the *title* of Biggest Liar belonged to Joe Biden."

"Except that Hillary was 100% aware of everything she did."

"Didn't Bill and Hillary die within days of one another?"

"Two, to be exact. Now, he hangs out with Jeffery Epstein, and she's still trying to figure out how to dethrone Nancy, who got there first, and be the Queen of Hell. As a matter of fact, her name in Hell is no longer Hillary, it's Lilith. And going back to my mischievous ways, it's pretty funny to watch her continually bump her head on the glass ceiling that I put up as a joke. It's unbreakable glass. But, enough of that. Let's stick to the plan.

Censorship is probably the biggest tool employed by the NEW WORLD ORDER, the DEMOCRATIC PARTY, and the BIDEN ADMINISTRATION. And it comes in two forms. The first form is out-and-out censorship, as had been the plan for years. Their dictum was, and will be until the end of time:

Don't let them hear the truth.

Don't let them know the truth.

And at all cost, never let the truth get out.

The second form, was to make sure, in the event that something *did* get out, to use every tool imaginable to stop GOOD from exposing it.

I'll give you some interesting facts that you might not be aware of, and facts that the NEW WORLD ORDER, DEMOCRATIC PARTY, and JOE BIDEN ADMINISTRATION will do everything in their power to bury. There was a big shift in political leanings after Biden took office, meaning that if it were strictly Conservative vs. Liberal, Conservatives actually outnumbered Liberals by 12%. If you can get that 12% advantage, and hope that the Republican Party has spent their money in the right places, meaning as overseers at every polling place in America for starters, it will be a devastating blow to the NEW WORLD ORDER, DEMOCRATIC PARTY, and the JOE BIDEN ADMINISTRATION, and hopefully, with Donald Trump in office will be a springboard to the reversal of NEW WORLD ORDER and DEMOCRATIC PARTY policies and agenda, paving the road back to freedom, common sense, and sanity.

And *that*, above all, should be your goal. You must encourage and help those who have been imprisoned by the NEW WORLD ORDER and DEMOCRATIC PARTY propaganda machine to reclaim their conscience, reclaim their Common Sense, reclaim their Free Will, and do what is truly the best path for themselves, their families, their friends, and their country."

"12% is a huge difference."

"It's worth repeating what you're up against with the NEW WORLD ORDER, the DEMOCRATIC PARTY, and the BIDEN ADMINISTRATION. They will do everything in their power to stop you, or anyone else from exposing the truth.

To repeat one of the most important things to know about them, this is what they are unflinchingly dedicated to:

Don't let them hear the truth.
Don't let them know the truth.
And at all cost, never let the truth get out.

Because the Truth, which can only be enjoyed in a free and open society, is Kryptonite to the NEW WORLD ORDER, the DEMOCRATIC PARTY, and the BIDEN ADMINISTRATION."

"Remember, for the NEW WORLD ORDER, by any name since its inception, is all about CONTROL, CONTROL, CONTROL. You are now aware of the UNITED NATIONS 2021 Agenda, and the 2030 Agenda, but the UNITED NATIONS and NEW WORLD ORDER weren't finished. The UNITED NATIONS also moved to radicalize the world banking system under the Central Bank Digital Currency (CBDC), with a new "unified ledger" proposal that had been published by the Bank of International Settlements (BIS), known as the "bank of banks." Together, this new, centralized NEW WORLD ORDER-controlled unified ledger tokenized all financial assets to rule them from a globalist database that they altered to meet their needs, at any time. And it controlled real estate, bank accounts, stocks, and pension funds. The list went on and on, and the governments of the world just let it happen."

"It's almost unfathomable that so many could just not care; not care about themselves, their family, their friends, and their country. No matter what my goal or mission is, I guess I'll never understand why people have this need to think they must dominate everyone else."

"It's definitely a human thing. But it's real. It's interesting, from my perspective anyway that the megalomaniacs of history have all thought it was their destiny to conquer the entire world. From as far back as Julius Caesar, Alexander, Napolean, Hitler, and to Xi Jinping, they all believed that their military power would be the answer to conquering the world. But the NEW WORLD ORDER, in and unto itself, has never been a military power. They have controlled various armies of the world, but it has always been about outthinking and out-planning their adversaries.

Here's another huge example of outthinking your opposers, enemies, or even your supposed allies. Once the NEW WORLD ORDER got unfettered control of the American federal government and most of the state governments, by controlling elections, they used everything in their arsenal to make all of the citizens dependent on them- food shortages, energy shortages, and the Pandemic of 2029 that wiped out hundreds of millions worldwide.

But to make it happen, their biggest coup, and most necessary coup, was indoctrinating the American military that the citizenry was the enemy, and the NEW WORLD ORDER government were the good guys. All they needed were a few brainwashed generals to lead the way and the military just followed along. They took away all of the guns in the hands of everyday citizens, and then began the genocide of millions, starting with their biggest political threats, the homeless, then the elderly, and from there anyone who wouldn't surrender to them."

"Obviously I saw and experienced all of it. But I was always baffled why the FBI never questioned their orders to raid the homes of political opponents of JOE BIDEN and the DEMOCRATIC PARTY."

"The short answer is that the agents they used to do the raids were already vetted, and known to be Leftist disciples of the vision of the NEW WORLD ORDER. Couple that with orders from a demagogue FBI Director, and supported by orders from Himmler, I'm sorry, Garland, and you had all that was needed to carry out the raids."

"Stop!"

"What now?"

"Even I know who Himmler was. But why the reference to Biden's Attorney General, Merrick Garland?"

"It wasn't *my* reference. It was Himmler's reference."

"Please explain."

"The short version is this- Himmler was ten times more demented than Hitler ever thought of being. He believed in the occult, was realistically the driving force behind the Mass Formation Psychosis that made Jews the target of the Holocaust, and he also believed in reincarnation. He's sitting in Hell, as we speak, bragging to his co-conspirator disciples who went to Hell with him that his legacy lives on with his reincarnation in the form of Merrick Garland."

"Is that true?"

"*Himmler* believes it. True or not, imagine what your world would have been like if Garland had made it to the Supreme Court."

Traveler, without losing a breath, continued.

"Under BIDEN, there were twelve who were raided, including the public assault at Mar-a-Lago and Donald Trump. Trump wasn't actually arrested, so raped might be a more accurate description. And then there are the dozens who sat in prison in violation of the US Constitution for almost two years for taking part in the January 6 protest. There were two more arrests of religious leaders who dared to be a part of Pro-Life rallies and participate in a non-violent sit-in. Every one of these were purposeful, to make people scared to speak out.

They carried out those raids and arrested those people as if each and every one of the arrestees were domestic terrorists who had participated in mass killings or bombings.

If the JUSTICE DEPARTMENT and the BIDEN ADMINISTRATION boldly carried out these raids in BIDEN's first term, why was anyone surprised at what BIDEN's successor, meaning the Closer, was able to do after the 2024 election?

Surprisingly, all of this took place with the blessing and encouragement of the Chinese Communists, with the Chinese thinking all along that by having the NEW WORLD ORDER make total wusses out of American soldiers, and eliminating their training, they would be ill-equipped to go up against an army of millions. The Chinese truly believed that the NEW WORLD ORDER was their biggest asset, all the while believing that they would someday bring the NEW WORLD ORDER under their domain, using their army to do so.

But the NEW WORLD ORDER was way ahead of them, with a pathogen that was specific to the Chinese genome. Artificial Intelligence did the rest. No one ever knew exactly how many Chinese died in the pandemic of 2031, but for the record it was close to 8 million, which doesn't sound like much in a country of one-and-a-half billion. However, the 8 million were specific to the government and military. The NEW WORLD ORDER simply cut the head off the snake and watched the body dry up, turn to dust, and blow away."

"In 2031? I wasn't aware of any of that happening."

"How would you or anyone else know anything unless they wanted you to know, which they didn't, so they simply suppressed the story."

"Eight million Chinese?"

"And counting, in 2036, though it's wasn't necessary. China in 2036 resembled China in 1936 more than anything. Imagine if China had simply wanted to be a four-walled country that was only interested in being left alone, and therefore leaving everyone else alone? The NEW WORLD ORDER probably would have left them alone. But Xi Jinping's narcissism made him just like the hierarchy of the NEW WORLD ORDER, so he and China had to go."

"The more I get to know, the more I realize that you're right. Americans are suckers."

"Sad but true. But it happened, nonetheless, because the lies and propaganda of the NEW WORLD ORDER are very strong. They continually pointed the finger at GOOD, and successfully convinced enough of their brainwashed followers that GOOD was evil, and EVIL was good."

Traveler let everything soak in, allowing Chelsea to try and regroup in her mind all of the information, and what could be done with it.

"The most important thing to remember, that will hopefully keep you on task, is this - If the NEW WORLD ORDER cannot be stopped in the 2024 presidential election, it's game-over for the United States, and the world."

"Was Global Warming real?"
"Define Global Warming."

Chelsea thought about it for a while in Earth-time, before answering.

"Um, Global Warming, is…Global Warming."
"That's exactly the kind of answer I would expect from the mind of a six-year-old, or a devotee of the NEW WORLD ORDER and the DEMOCRATIC PARTY, which were pretty much the same."
"I'm sorry, but I honestly don't know *what* Global Warming actually was."
"If it will make you feel any better, neither did they, meaning those who were fueling the Mass Formation Psychosis talking points of the NEW WORLD ORDER and the DEMOCRATIC PARTY. In 2024 the mindless moron-drones of the NEW WORLD ORDER didn't know what Global Warming was, nor what, *from the River to the Sea* meant, but they continued to scream it out from the rooftops whenever they had the opportunity."

Chelsea had a befuddled countenance, which again, amused Traveler.

"I already know what that look means. I'll explain it later. For starters, yes, the Earth was getting warmer since they started measuring it in 1900. By the time you died in 2036 the temperature of the Artic had risen by about thirty-two degrees in one-hundred-thirty-six years."
"That's a lot."

"I won't disagree. But it wasn't about what was actually happening, it was about who they wanted you to believe was responsible for it happening. It was a political football, with the NEW WORLD ORDER and the DEMOCRATIC PARTY effectively using it against anyone who wasn't on board with their propaganda machine to *Go Green*, which as everyone came to discover was another NEW WORLD ORDER propaganda campaign. What's interesting is that it was never about the actual warming. What it was, was the NEW WORLD ORDER and the DEMOCRATIC PARTY continually creating *Chicken Little* drama so that their followers never had time to stop and think about anything except that which was being fed to them on a daily basis. They needed to always control the narrative, about anything and everything. It what makes Mass Formation Psychosis so easy to accomplish."

"Is it worth talking about?"

"No. It's a non-starter, as they say. And it's not a hot-topic issue in the Presidential election in 2024."

"But it was real?"

"Tell you what. When you go back, and if you manage to save the world, I'll tell you the real reasons for Global Warming and how to fix it."

"Not even a hint?"

Traveler loved that he always had the answers to any question, but was hesitant to get involved in this issue as it wouldn't help her. Nonetheless, he dangled the answer in front of her. " It really started to escalate in the 1990s."

"That's it?... And you can fix it?"

"Oh, ye of little faith...."

"Everything you've told me so far shows how the NEW WORLD ORDER took over the world. But I know it's going to come up, often, and I'm not prepared just yet for the questions and challenges about the 2020 election."

"In 2020, when the NEW WORLD ORDER flexed its muscles for all to see, and won the battle of wills, meaning the Republican Party caved, dropping the challenges to the election results in a few states. What do you remember about the election?"

"To be honest, not much, except that it appeared that Donald Trump had been elected, and before you knew it he was unelected, and Biden was President of the United States. In retrospect, I have to admit that I had no idea that one person could take the greatest country in the world and reduce it to ashes in such a short time."

"Not that it makes it any better or easier to accept but he had a lot of help. Think about it. In the primary season, Joe Biden, in what was his fourth attempt to be President, was out of the primaries and almost a forgotten memory until he suddenly got resurrected in South Carolina. And then he was ordered to pick an almost arch-enemy rival, Kamala Harris, as his running mate."

"No one I knew could believe it."

"It is if you understand the concept of a Manchurian Candidate. A Manchurian candidate is a person, especially a politician, being used as a puppet by an enemy power. The term is commonly used to indicate disloyalty or corruption, whether intentional or unintentional."

"I've heard the expression, and I think I actually saw the movie, but I'm still not sure what it means."

"Skipping to the original book, it's the story about a POW who spent way too much time as a POW, especially when he had the opportunity to come home, and points directly at John McCain, which may or may not be a story for another time. It shows how a presidential candidate who could have easily won, willingly threw the election, and as a result Barack Obama became president; a concept that is easy to see by some and hard to accept by most."

"You must know. Did that actually happen?"

"It will have no bearing on your book, so let's stick with Joe Biden, Manchurian Candidate for the NEW WORLD ORDER. By virtue of his willingness to dismiss and forego much of his beliefs, and do the bidding of the NEW WORLD ORDER, in trade for getting a wish that not even a genie could have given him-the Presidency, Joe Biden checked all of the boxes."

"As long as you put it that way, you'll get no argument from me."

"All Joe Biden had to do at that point was sit in his bunker and let the NEW WORLD ORDER and DEMOCRATIC PARTY do the rest. Do you remember that before Joe Biden and Donald Trump debated, that Donald Trump wanted drug tests for both candidates? Do you remember that the NEW WORLD ORDER immediately started a campaign to deflect Trump's request, trying to make everyone think that it was *not* about Biden's mental state?"

"You know, yes, I do remember that. You mean that they already suspected in 2020 that Biden's brain was *going*?"

"Yes and No. Yes, his brain was already going, which is why Trump wanted the drug test. Trump's team had been secretly informed that the NEW WORLD ORDER was already experimenting with different drugs to boost Biden's energy, mental state, and overall performance. But, as usual, the NEW WORLD ORDER won the argument and no test was ever done. Nevertheless, once they got by the debates it was getting too risky to keep him juiced all the time, so they simply hid Biden in the basement and ran his campaign through surrogates, namely CNN and Social Media platforms."

"Did Trump really win, meaning the NEW WORLD ORDER and the DEMOCRATIC PARTY successfully change the election results, as was widely accepted?"

"Let me refer back to where I told you that everything you say or do has to be verifiable. But, you have now entered a gray area. What I personally know is one thing. What most Americans are sure happened but can't prove is another thing. Without a mountain of proof, either in the form of documents or sworn testimony, there is no *verifiable* proof. But, what there is, is the Science of Statistics, that could still be a very useful tool, if by no other means than to get people *thinking* that it is the only logical answer."

"How can I do that?"

"There was a man in your home state of California who used the Science of Statistics and Deductive Reasoning to prove that the election *must* have been stolen, without ever coming out and saying it. He left the final decision to the person listening to the statistics he had provided, and simply asked, at the end, 'So, what do you think is the logical conclusion?'"

"What were these statistics?"

"This man would start his explanation by emphasizing the obviousness of the purity of mathematics. No one has ever disputed that numbers don't lie, and as a result, often-times it becomes necessary to point you away from the numbers to avoid simple conclusions."

"Please get to the point. I'm not a mathematician."

"Stating the obvious, for starters, was that all elections in America were reliant on polling, when polling was allowed. Congressional races, senatorial races, and especially the presidential races were subject to daily scrutiny by different polling organizations and press outlets who tried to skew even the plainest of results to favor one candidate or another. Interview two thousand, and report the results of only one thousand respondents to drive the message. If your candidate was behind, don't ever admit how far behind, or people would stay home and not vote."

"Yes, I knew how that worked. I also remember that in 2016, 90% of the polls said that Hillary was going to beat Trump, hoping that Trump voters would stay home because it would be a waste of time to vote for Trump."

"Well, luckily the Trump voters didn't believe the greatest political liar in the history of the United States, and got out and voted. And you just said something that is the basis of the proof of what really happened in the 2020 election."

"I did?"

"Yes. What do all presidential polls have in common?"

Traveler couldn't wait- "They're involuntary."

"No they're not. People offer the information."

"But only after they've been caught off guard on a street corner or on the telephone. Yes, most tell the truth, but some didn't, out of fear of retaliation. But suppose that there had been a voluntary poll?"

"A voluntary poll? What's a voluntary poll?"

"A voluntary poll is one in which the participants, without any outside pressure or influence, whatsoever, volunteer their support for the candidate of their choice."

"I'm not aware of any such poll."

"Actually you are. As a matter of fact, I happen to know that you participated."

"I know that you know everything there is to know about me, but I was *never* in a voluntary poll."

"Or so you thought. You see, this is where the man from California would catch most people off guard. He would go on to say, '...and suppose, just suppose, that this poll wasn't just one thousand people, or ten thousand, or even a million. Suppose that this poll had over 108 million participants?'"

"I think I would have been very aware of such a poll, and I wasn't."

"But there was, and you were. And no one was more scared of the statistics from that poll than the NEW WORLD ORDER and the DEMOCRATIC PARTY."

Chelsea shook her head, and shrugged her shoulders, clearly indicating that she was still not understanding what he was talking about.

"How come this is the first I've ever heard of this man's analysis of the election?"

"Because he never pushed the narrative hard enough. There was too much against him. But you can."

"What were his conclusions?"

"To cut to the chase, this poll provided an irrefutable fact, and a gauge, of Trump supporters vs. Biden supporters to show and predict that Biden didn't have a prayer to win the election; that Biden would have been lucky to have gotten elected president of his hometown garden society, let alone President of the United States. And to prove it, all anyone had to do was take a look at the voluntary poll - Twitter."

"Twitter? What about Twitter?"

"A week before the election, Trump had 88.8 million followers, and Biden had 20 million. Now, please keep in mind that Twitter followers are *voluntary*. They become a *follower* because it is a way of showing support."

"That's quite a difference."

"Enough that it scared the NEW WORLD ORDER and the DEMOCRATIC PARTY to the point of hysteria. And when the NEW WORLD ORDER and the DEMOCRATIC PARTY saw what happened in Pennsylvania the week before the election, they knew they didn't have a choice but to resort to illicit means to steal the election."

"I don't remember anything happening."

"A week before the election, in Pennsylvania, Trump had four rallies in one day. 100,000 people showed up. Within days of the Trump rallies, Biden did *one* rally in Philadelphia, supposedly his stronghold in Pennsylvania. Only 2,000 showed up, and that included all of the media and their crews. Did you ever see the Fake News outlets show the crowds? Did you ever see a crowd behind Biden cheering him on? Did you ever see anyone, even in California wearing a Biden hat or t-shirt? The answer is *never*, because Biden had the least enthusiastic campaign of supporters in the history of the country. And the numbers had been growing for Trump for months, but not for Biden."

"Biden only had 20 million Twitter followers?"

"Amazing, isn't it? And, as they say, numbers don't lie, but propaganda absolutely lies, and is the most-used tool of the NEW WORLD ORDER and the DEMOCRATIC PARTY. The man's first point was, how could Trump have 88.8 million followers and only get 74 million votes in the most important election of the times? He further stated that the 88.8 million number was probably low, as many of the followers had multiple supporters in each house.

The best question he asked was: *How are we to believe that in the most important election of our lifetime that 14 million Trump supporters decided to stay home and not vote?*"

"So, Trump had over 88 million followers and got only 74 million votes. And Biden got how many?"

"Biden got 80 million votes, and only had 20 million followers. Just to be clear- Trump would have had to have had 14 million avid followers stay home and *not* vote, and Biden would have had to have found 60 million more followers for the election to suddenly decide to get out and vote."

"That seems impossible. Those kinds of numbers are pretty hard to argue with."

"Exactly. But it is the propaganda that the NEW WORLD ORDER, the DEMOCRATIC PARTY, and the BIDEN CAMPAIGN needed everyone to believe. And keep in mind that they weren't pushing that *either narrative* was an explanation of the Biden win. They pushed the narrative that *both* things happened, simultaneously."

"And they got away with it. But how?"

"Because the NEW WORLD ORDER, the DEMOCRATIC PARTY, and the BIDEN CAMPAIGN controlled 90% of the media outlets in the country, and enough of the hierarchy in the JUSTICE DEPARTMENT and the FBI to run just enough interference to control the narrative.

To pour more gasoline onto the fire, here is what the NEW WORLD ORDER, the DEMOCRATIC PARTY, and the BIDEN CAMPAIGN successfully buried, which was in keeping with the statistics that proved that Joe Biden would have been lucky to get elected as Dog Catcher in his hometown."

"Wait. I thought you said President of the Garden Society."

"Take your pick. To continue...How was it that Donald Trump, an incumbent President with a robust economy the likes that had never been seen in modern times, lost Arizona, Georgia, Michigan, Pennsylvania, and Wisconsin; states that he had won only four years before, in 2016? ALL of them were states that showed he had won on election night 2020. ALL were states that delayed the official vote count until such time as mysterious ballots showed up to show that he had *not* won. ALL were states led by DEMOCRATIC PARTY governors. Now, common sense dictates that there was a possibility that, maybe, the Democrats could have flipped one of those states. But all five?"

"I never heard anyone put all of these facts into one, nice little bundle. When you consider the Twitter followers, and the five states that flipped and shouldn't have, it begs the question: How could Americans be so stupid to let this narrative play out?"

"And yet they did. It might be a slight stretch, but from a statistics standpoint, a person would have a better chance at winning the lottery, twice in the same week, without ever buying a ticket than to have all of the things happen in the 2020 Presidential Election that gave Biden the Presidency. But that is exactly what the NEW WORLD ORDER, the DEMOCRATIC PARTY, and the BIDEN CAMPAIGN sold, and enough Americans bought.

To repeat - Always be aware that numbers don't lie, but propaganda does, and the NEW WORLD ORDER and the DEMOCRATIC PARTY are the masters of propaganda."

"Question- How can you win the lottery without buying a ticket?"

"By accepting hyperbole, in your case, or just being a member of the upper echelon of the NEW WORLD ORDER."

"Am I biting off more than I can chew in taking on the NEW WORLD ORDER and the DEMOCRATIC PARTY?"

"What do you have to lose? You're already dead."

"It was too bad the United States never found a better voting system than the Electoral College. And it was always the Democrats who complained. If they won they were happy and didn't care. But if they lost, especially if they lost the Electoral College and won the popular vote, we never heard the end of it."

"I must say that I certainly understand the argument. Which is why, over the years I have witnessed many verbal challenges to the Electoral College system, but the only alternative has been going to the popular vote. But even *that* would open the door to fraud and confusion, with the fraud being too hard to trace, as to where it happened."

"Is there another alternative?"

"Oddly enough, the same person who pointed out the statistical challenge to the 2020 election, and the Gruesome Newsom recall fiasco in California, which we will talk about next, once also mentioned a solution to the Electoral College system. He called it the Congressional District Voting System, which combined the Electoral System and the Popular Vote System into a system that would appease both camps."

"The same man?"

"The same man."

" What made him come up with it?"

"He actually thought of it after the Bush-Gore election of 2000. If his idea had been in place, the Florida debacle would have never occurred. Consequently, in 2020, if it had been in place, Donald Trump would have had a better argument for a vote count challenge as it would have been specific to congressional districts and not to an entire state. If you are familiar with the Electoral College System, it is easy to understand how it works. Take your home state of California for instance. It has 52 Congressional Districts and 54 Electoral Votes. The key is, that California is a *winner take all* state when it comes to electoral votes. What that does, in effect, is disenfranchise so many Conservative voters because they know that the Democrats substantially outnumber them in the large cities, which is enough votes to win the entire state. It's the same in other states where Liberals and Democrats are feeling the same frustration. But suppose that it wasn't a winner take all state, or in any other state for that matter?

The Congressional District Voting System gives one vote to each and every congressional district. There are 435 congressional districts, and each one is required to be equal in population, as closely as possible, to all other congressional districts in the same state. Basically, what it means is that the candidate who gets the most votes in the congressional district, gets that district's vote. It's that simple. 218 votes wins the presidency.

Under the Congressional District Voting System, voters are more inclined to vote, knowing that their vote actually counts, and is not subject to the entire electoral college vote for a state that is at the mercy of large urban areas. The advantage of the system is really in the event of a dispute. If there were a questionable vote count, under the Congressional District Voting System, it would be specific to the congressional district, and not to the entire state. Truly, it's a win-win."

"Were there any other examples of voting fraud, like we saw in the 2020 election, statistically speaking?"

"A few here and there in senatorial and gubernatorial races. And a major-city mayoral race in your home state of California. Just keep in mind one fact. If the vote counting suddenly gets dragged out and they can't call an election in a couple of days, then the fix is in, and the NEW WORLD ORDER and DEMOCRATIC PARTY are behind it. But the next example should be even more interesting. It involves the recall election of Governor Newsom in your home state of California.

"They did it again?"

"Oh, they did more than that. They pushed the limits of their crimes to a whole new level, and still got away with it."

"Is this from you or did the information come from a human source?"

"Actually, this analysis comes from the same man in California who pointed out the impossibility, statistically, of Biden winning the presidency, and the introduction of the Congressional District Voting System."

"This guy sounds like he was more guilty of doing nothing than I was."

"I know that he's of the mindset that if *you* win, he wins, and everyone wins."

"How will I know it's him if I run into him?"

"He firmly believes and prays for the possibility that someone like you will suddenly appear, so he won't be surprised, even if you tell him who you are. As the saying goes, *he's got a lot of skin in the game.*"

"Okay, let's have it."

"Shortly after the recall election of Gavin Newsom, on September 20, 2021, the man we're talking about wrote a letter to Larry Elder, the person who would have been governor, providing the evidence that Newsom lost the election by almost 2 million votes."

"Two million?! That can't be. The State published the results."

"And right there, out in the open for everyone to see. But according to the person who wrote the letter, no one ever *analyzed* the results. Everyone just accepted what the State of California told them. Sound familiar?"

"You mean like when they told us what Trump said on the bus, but he didn't say it."

"Exactly. What makes this different from the 2020 election *statistical supposition* is that these were the actual numbers provided by the State of California. According to the facts in the letter, … You know what? Just read the letter, and then we'll talk about it."

"Do you know where the letter is?"

"Seriously?"

Traveler handed her the letter, and she began to read it aloud.

Dear Mr. Elder:

In the California election on September 14, 2021, Governor Gavin Newsom was forced into a recall election by the voters of California. The recall election was in two parts/questions. Question #1 asked voters to choose "YES" or "NO" on whether Newsom should be recalled. If you thought Newsom should remain in office, vote "NO." If you thought Gavin Newsom should be removed from office, vote "YES."

Question #1 is what the Secretary of State, the Board of Elections, the Newsom campaign, and the Democratic Party want us to concentrate on, and also for us to conveniently dismiss the second question, which was to vote for the candidate of your choice to replace Newsom in Question #2. To push the narrative, they concentrated on percentages, and not actual numbers when publishing the results.

You can use whatever term(s) you want, be it Forensic Analysis, Analytical Method, the Science of Statistical Analysis, or plain old Common Sense, but the final outcome will be the same – based on the hard numbers, it's impossible that Gavin Newsom survived the recall effort. As a matter of fact, the numbers support the notion that Newsom got trounced, and Larry Elder should have been elected Governor of California.

The CERTIFIED RESULTS, per the California Secretary of State, are as follows:

- 12,838,565 votes were cast in the election.

- NO votes were 61.9%, meaning the recall failed. Total votes = 7,944,092.

- YES votes were 38.1%. Total votes = 4,894,473.

- 7,400,000 votes were cast (Question #2) for various candidates to replace Newsom, with Larry Elder clearly the winner.

- 5.5 million Voters left their ballots blank on the question of who should take Newsom's place if the recall passed.

But as we all know, the numbers are the numbers, and numbers don't lie. So, what can we deduce and conclude from the numbers in the CERTIFIED RESULTS?

The first conclusion is actually a "given," meaning that no one who voted NO, meaning the voters who wanted to reject the recall and keep Newsom in office, would have voted for an alternate candidate in Question #2. As a matter of fact, Newsom's campaign spent a fortune telling his supporters to avoid voting for an alternate candidate, in Question #2, and to concentrate on simply voting NO on Question #1. Therefore, it makes sense that the number of "blank" ballots on Question #2 should have been equal to the number of NO votes in Question #1. It means that the number of

Question #2 "blank" ballots should have been 7,944,092, and not 5,500,000. That's a difference of 2,444,092 votes. Simply put, why the huge discrepancy and what does it mean?

To understand it better, and more to the point, consider the reverse analysis of the vote count- 7,400,000 votes were cast for alternate candidates in Question #2, to choose a new governor, if and when the recall had been successful.

Why would voters cast 7,400,000 votes for someone else to be governor, but, according to the official results, only cast 4,894,473 votes to recall Newsom? Are we to believe that 2,505,527 pro-recall voters failed to vote YES in Question #1? Are we to concurrently believe that the 2,505,527 votes in question were cast as NO votes? Does that make any sense, to anyone?

The purpose of voting for an alternate candidate was reliant on getting Newsom recalled in Question #1. To that end, an equal number of votes must have been cast to recall Newsom (YES votes), as there were for alternate candidates. That number is irrefutably, 7,400,000. There would not have been any purpose in showing up to vote for an alternate candidate if a voter hadn't also been there to cast a YES vote in Question #1.

Both analyses support the conclusion that the vote count is suspicious at least, and totally bogus at best.

Simple mathematics recalculates what we've been told about the vote tallies in Question #1.

- **YES votes actually totaled…..7,400,000 (57.6%).**
- **NO votes actually totaled……5,438,565 (42.4%)**

In consideration of a 2%-5% variance, per the Science of Statistics, it would allow for a remote possibility that some people may have forgotten to vote to recall Newsom. Even so, it still would not have been a close vote.

Numbers don't lie, and Common Sense should prevail. ***Newsom should have been recalled, losing by 1,961,435 votes."***

Chelsea put the letter down.

"I can't believe this. It's all right here. They lied, again."

"And quite successfully I might add. They gave everyone the numbers, and then simply delivered a false narrative as to what votes were actually cast, and for whom."

"It definitely reminds me of the Trump-on-the-bus lie. And they got away with it because we sat back and let them."

"Most definitely. They got away with it over and over. The mayoral election in Los Angeles, Governor of Arizona, Senator from Arizona… It happened everywhere. I heard someone say, after the LA mayor's race:

Why doesn't someone just walk the streets of Los Angeles with a camera and microphone asking people who they voted for, for mayor? Not only would they say that they voted for Caruso, but I'd be willing to bet they couldn't even tell you the name of the person who supposedly ran against Caruso, and won.

Chelsea dropped her head in disgust.

"I'm embarrassed."

"You should be."

"What else am I missing?"

"There are a few more things that you should be aware of, and how they play into the plan of the NEW WORLD ORDER, DEMOCRATIC PARTY, and JOE BIDEN vision of a world takeover. They are areas where the NEW WORLD ORDER, DEMOCRATIC PARTY, and JOE BIDEN ADMINISTRATION have effectively used the power of Social Media and Mainstream Media outlets to continually bombard Americans with Mass Formation Psychosis on a number of different subjects. We're not going to go into them in depth, but a simple discussion of each should be enough.

"Infinite striving to be the best is man's duty; it is its own reward. Everything else is in God's hands."
— Gandhi

"Meritocracy is the notion of a socio-political system in which individual people, and their successes, are based on talent, effort, performance, and demonstrated achievement. It has been that way in America since Day 1.

Conservatives value the concept of Meritocracy, but Liberals do not. As a matter of verifiable fact, not only do Liberals not like it, but they insult many of its base of supporters in doing so. What does it say to any ethnic group when you say to them, *I know you aren't smart, and you will never get ahead in the world, so I am going to lower the standards so it appears that you are smart.*

Conservatives will say, *I know you're as smart as anyone else, and I'm going to help you prove it by helping you with a better education.*

In 2024 alone, states like Oregon were abandoning a Bar examination for a person to be allowed to practice law. The SATs were being *tweaked* so that underachieving students would score better. The Liberals who are running these programs aren't too far off from saying, *Oh, you're a taxidermist? You know, with your skills you could make a lot more money if you just became a heart surgeon.*

Meritocracy makes all of us better by making us strive to be better. But the NEW WORLD ORDER, the DEMOCRATIC PARTY, and JOE BIDEN ADMINISTRATION want everyone to abandon the principles of Meritocracy and simply let them, meaning the NEW WORLD ORDER, take care of you. Remember the first promise of the GREAT RESET? *You will own nothing and be happy!"*

"October 2024, as you undoubtedly remember, was branded *The Bloody "O."* The NEW WORLD ORDER was happy that the world accepted its meaning as the Bloody October. But to the NEW WORLD ORDER it was their final pre-election push to install their puppet, meaning the Closer, into the White House for what would be the final, seemingly legitimate presidential election of the United States. Behind closed doors, they called it the Bloody Overthrow.

For most of the election season the NEW WORLD ORDER had been playing their usual game of *disinformation,* skewing every poll imaginable to make it look like Biden was still well-within the margin of error to win, and generally eliminating RFK Jr. from the equation to keep up appearances. They knew that the gap between Trump and Biden wasn't even close. Trump was up by at least 20% in most states, including the supposed toss-up states. The plan, by doing so, was to make another election theft seem plausible by keeping the race appear, close. Though the RNC and the Trump camp knew about the Ploy, meaning that Biden was about to get slaughtered, nonetheless they let the margins publicly stay close in order to strengthen the support of the Republican base and create a situation for the narrative that every vote would be critical, and thus encouraging more people to vote.

However, as you may recall, RFK's momentum was growing, getting much support from Democrats who objected to the DEMOCRATIC PARTY and the BIDEN ADMINISTRATION trying to keep Kennedy off the state ballots and off the stage for the two planned debates. But when RFK got onto the ballot in several states, including Arizona, Nevada, and Georgia, the problem was that when the NEW WORLD ORDER had planned to steal those states for a second time, RFK's position on the ballot changed everything. When RFK got onto the ballot in Michigan, the NEW WORLD ORDER and the DEMOCRATIC PARTY knew the deck had actually been stacked against them for the planned ballot theft. Panic set in.

After Biden clearly lost the first debate, the DEMOCRATIC PARTY and the BIDEN ADMINISTRATION tried using every excuse imaginable to not participate in the second debate, but with a debate already planned, Trump agreed to debate RFK instead. The NEW WORLD ORDER, the DEMOCRATIC PARTY, and the BIDEN camp went ballistic, realizing that giving RFK the stage was tantamount to brushing BIDEN aside and out of consideration. And that is exactly what happened.

Within days of the Trump/RFK debate, Biden's numbers had *publicly* slipped beyond any chance of recovery. It was clear that the NEW WORLD ORDER candidate, Joe Biden, was going to get annihilated in the November 5 election. The NEW WORLD ORDER decided to put it all on the line. To remind you, the date was October 2, 2024. At a rally, reminiscent of the rally at the Ambassador Hotel in Los Angeles in 1968, a crazed gunman with an assault rifle was able to spray the event with 24 shots before being killed by security.

RFK Jr. and six others died in the attack, and the NEW WORLD ORDER smiled in approval."

"I remember it well."

"And then the NEW WORLD ORDER went on a propaganda campaign to explain that it was RFK's destiny to die that way, and that no one should question what was obviously, and simply, his fate.

With Kennedy out of the race, the NEW WORLD ORDER and the DEMOCRATIC PARTY got another surprise- Biden's numbers didn't recover, in spite of a disinformation campaign reigniting the anti-assault weapons agenda, which again would be a key ingredient of taking away the guns of patriots who would be willing to fight to the end to defend freedom.

With the obviousness of Biden losing big, Biden suddenly was complaining of ailments that no one would question. So, he pardoned his son, Hunter, of all crimes and stepped down as President. Kamala, saying that she suddenly had no desire to be President, or publicly eliminated, also stepped down, and the NEW WORLD ORDER candidate stepped up to the plate, all the while reminding everyone that he never desired to be President but felt obligated to run to keep America free from Donald Trump. His name didn't matter. The world simply knew him as the *Closer*.

"I watched all of that happen. So, now it's my challenge to make it *not*-happen."

"That's the plan. And I can tell you that you will be in the fight of your life. If you have learned anything, it should be that the NEW WORLD ORDER is not just capable of anything, but will *do* anything to achieve their ultimate goal of total world domination and the destruction of Man on Earth, as it has been known since God first created Adam. You will see, hear, and experience Mass Formation Psychosis, the Wrap-up Smear, and a MOB mentality, of and by the NEW WORLD ORDER and its subsidiaries on a scale never witnessed before. They will be in an all-or-nothing mode, and capable of just about anything you can imagine."

"Is it possible they could push up the release of the 2029 Pandemic?"

"They are certainly capable of it. But first they will release the Bird-Flu that was originally released in 2026. Then lock down the country and delay the election to give them more time to plan on getting rid of Donald Trump."

"What about me, if I happen to be successful?"

"You will also be in their crosshairs. And you will recognize the tactics, as I know that you are very familiar with the Salem Witch Trials where the mass hysteria of the MOB, created by the simple pointing of a finger resulted in trials of more than two-hundred, and the hanging of nineteen. Clearly, EVIL were not those that hanged but EVIL was most definitely the people who hanged them. Make no mistake about it- the NEW WORLD ORDER will be pointing the finger, and you will be their Witch."

Traveler didn't mind that Chelsea was allowing him to ramble, but he was concerned as to what degree that she was grasping and absorbing all that he had to teach. Obviously she was taking copious notes, though it wasn't clear what she planned to do with them.

"How exactly do you plan to use the things that we have been talking about?"

"I haven't decided yet. I'm still wondering how much the average person would like to hear about all of these things we've been discussing. It's quite a bit to take in, even for me."

"I warned you about that. Yet, you seem to be taking detailed notes, non-stop. Are you planning on using all of it?"

"I plan on reading everything you say, editing it and shortening it so I can get the most amount of facts in the shortest amount of space. So, on whatever subject you decide to explore, just give it your all and then I'll decide later how much of it to use. "

"I'm fine with that…Heh, it's your book."

"What's next?"

"There are several areas of concern for voters in 2024, and the NEW WORLD ORDER has their hands in all of them. I will simply cover them, one at a time, and we'll see what happens."

"I'm good with that. You just talk, and I'll listen. If I have questions along the way, I'll call for a time-out. What's first?"

"By the end of 2024, federal, state, and local government handouts to ILLEGAL IMMIGRANTS topped $800,000,000,000 (eight hundred **billion** dollars). To put it into better perspective, that was the same amount of money needed to hand every American citizen, of all ages, almost $2,500 (twenty-five hundred dollars) each. And that is only what the BIDEN ADMINISTRATION, the NEW WORLD ORDER, and the DEMOCRATIC PARTY are admitting to. Stop complaining!!! *You will own nothing and be happy.* Remember?

When Donald Trump was President, he promised to build a wall on the Southern border, letting everyone know that if you wanted to come to America, legally, there was a process. As a result, illegal immigration was at its lowest levels in decades. And he accomplished this in spite of every DEMOCRAT in the Congress and Senate trying to stop him, using the term *xenophobia* as the rallying cry of the MASS FORMATION PSYCHOSIS propaganda tool of the NEW WORLD ORDER.

When Joe Biden came into office, he immediately stopped the building of the wall and opened up the border to all who wanted to come, including those who were let out of jail in their home countries, as long as they agreed to go to the United States, where Joe Biden would happily allow them to enter.

What happened then? I think everyone knows the answers, and that includes the WOKE morons who blindly followed the NEW WORLD ORDER, the DEMOCRATIC PARTY, and the JOE BIDEN ADMINISTATION. Crime, in every category, including murder, rape, assault, robbery, theft, and car-jackings immediately flew off the charts. Drugs, like Fentanyl, poured across the border and were the reason for thousands of deaths amongst the younger generations.

- Trillions of dollars (the BIDEN ADMINISTRATION will only admit to $800,000,000,000) were spent to support illegals at the federal, state, and local levels, by giving illegals free housing, free medical care, free clothing and food, and additional spending money, which many used to buy illegal guns and commit crimes.

- Illegals also set up a network to find vacant houses that are up for rent or sale, and illegally "squat" in those houses.

And while the NEW WORLD ORDER, the DEMOCRATIC PARTY, and the BIDEN ADMINISTRATION were spending trillions of taxpayer money to do this, it was taxpayers who suffered the consequences.

- They didn't care about American citizens living in poverty, who as Americans, could and should be getting the money that was going to illegal immigrants.

- They didn't care that the invasion of illegals played an important role in the escalating crime wave.

- They didn't care that the invasion of illegals played an important role in inflation.

- They didn't care that the invasion of illegals, meaning those who actually got a job, were replacing and forcing out people who already had those jobs, compelling those people being forced out of their jobs to take a huge cut in pay, go on unemployment, or take up a life of crime in order to feed themselves and their families.

- They didn't care that the invasion of illegals drove the cost of housing to the breaking point for most of the legal residents of America.

- They didn't care that food pieces soared to the point where shopping for basics was considered a luxury.

- They didn't care that gas prices were at unheard-of levels because Biden stopped the country's energy independence programs and started buying foreign oil.

- How interesting was it that BIDEN chose to buy Venezuelan oil of questionable quality, for much more than American oil would have cost.

- How interesting was it that the BIDEN IMMIGRATION agreement with Venezuela in 2022, in effect made it possible for Venezuelans to invade the United States. Did anyone ever ask how many Venezuelans were released from prison in Venezuela after being told to get out and go to America, where Joe Biden, the NEW WORLD ORDER and the DEMOCRATIC PARTY happily let them in?

It was no secret that the flood of illegals into the United States began on the first day of the BIDEN presidency. It was by design. Flooding the country with illegals was part of the destabilization plan for America by the NEW WORLD ORDER. The Illegals who invaded the United States were not only medically test-less and vaccine-less, but uneducated, and hungry. The hope and plan was that by being reliant on government subsidies to survive, the socialist approach to their well-being would make them *do* anything and *be* anything in order to stay, and to do as they're told.

To add fuel to the fire, in 2022 Senator Chuck Schumer derided Republicans for their *call to attention* about the NEW WORLD ORDER, DEMOCRATIC PARTY, and Joe Biden practice of *Replacement Theory*. Schumer publicly proclaimed that the Replacement Theory which he and the NEW WORLD ORDER, DEMOCRATIC PARTY, and JOE BIDEN AGENDA said was a conspiracy theory, was in fact real and accurate, saying that millions of illegals must be granted amnesty because the US population, '...is not producing on its own.'"

"Before discussing the actual act of Abortion, I want to point something out, which goes along with the NEW WORLD ORDER plan. After the Replacement Theory announcement by Schumer, the Senate Stooge of the NEW WORLD ORDER, no one connected some very important dots. Schumer proclaimed that the United States was not reproducing sufficiently on its own, and therefore illegals must be allowed in. Yet, for years he and the other Congressional mouthpieces of the NEW WORLD ORDER were pushing the pro-abortion agenda. So, out of one side of his mouth he was promoting open borders because the United States needed more people, and out of the other side of his mouth he was trying to pave the way for Americans to abort babies and *reduce* the population, using MASS FORMATION PSYCHOSIS to do it."

"Abortion was a tough one for me, because women, almost by default, were pro-abortion."

"Again, the result of Mass Formation Psychosis, which created the MOB, which created the problems."

"I stayed out of it. If and when the subject came up, which it often did amongst schoolteachers, I just thought it was easier to avoid hearing it and went to the bathroom."

"Smart move on one hand, and running from a fight on the other. If you run from a fight when you go back you'll never have a chance of convincing anyone of anything. Silence in opposition of anything, is not opposition. It is concession."

"It's an argument that can't be won."

"Then when it comes up, which it will, point the conversation in a different direction, to someplace in politics where there is more common ground, and therefore an opportunity to make some of the non-thinking-followers of EVIL into thinking-followers of Common Sense. If you can get them to that threshold, you're actually way beyond *half-way there*."

"What are your thoughts?"

"From a political perspective, and as someone who is a million times smarter than all of the justices combined who passed Roe vs, Wade in 1973, I can assure you that the Supreme Court of the United States got it absolutely *wrong*. In that ruling, the Supreme Court said that the US Constitution, by Adjudication, protected a woman's right to have an abortion."

"What does that mean?"

"Basically, that it was a *work-around* of the US Constitution. The US Constitution didn't apply specifically to the case, as abortion by name and definition wasn't even a consideration at the time the Constitution was written. They ignored the rights of the fathers under the Equal Protection Clause of the Constitution in order to appease the Pro-abortion Leftists who were gaining momentum and power at the time of the decision. And then they simply pushed it through."

"I never really paid attention to the legal aspects. I was simply adhering to the moral aspects."

"Which is how the confusion between the two, coupled with the "fetus viability" argument worked to keep it on the books for all of those years. Fetus viability is also the basis of the Leftist argument, to circumvent the Equal Protection Clause aspect, on behalf of the unborn child."

"About that... I knew a person, a fellow teacher, and a man whose wife had *their* baby aborted in the third month, without his prior knowledge. He went ballistic, which scared me, and her justification was, 'It's my body and my right. I can't do it right now because of the promotion, and I didn't want a baby standing in the way.' How sick was that?"

"It goes back to the Equal Protection Clause argument. If any government truly wanted to protect the rights of all concerned, an abortion should have required the signature of *both* parents before the abortion could be granted."

"Now, that actually makes sense... Okay, I like all of that. Now let me know what else you have to say on the subject."

"Just a quick thought and question. Why do you think that the pro-abortion people didn't want pro-life clinics anywhere near abortion centers?"

"I never thought about it."

"Because the pro-life people always wanted the mother to have an ultrasound, to actually see *how-formed* the baby was. *Not* wanting the mother to see the ultrasound is a prime example of one of the tenets of the NEW WORLD ORDER- Censorship."

"It's amazing how far they went."

"For the next 49 years the legal challenges and debates dominated the conversation, with anti-abortionists continually challenging the legality of Roe vs. Wade, at the very least on the federal level. In 2022 the Supreme Court got it right by determining that abortion is not a constitutional, *federally-protected* right. Consequently, the decision to have abortion on the books reverted back to the individual states."

"Why is it such a hot-topic issue?"

"It shouldn't be, as a presidential debate subject because it is no longer a *federal* issue. But the DEMOCRATIC PARTY needs it to be a front-and-center issue because it is the *only* unifying issue of the Liberal ideology. Abortion isn't just about abortion. Abortion is a rallying cry, but conversely it is the true test to prove that Liberals are basically just selfish, shallow, and illogical. They continued to support any candidate who wanted to federally reinstate Roe Vs. Wade, with little care or regard for the fact that the USA was economically and politically collapsing all around them.

But, as an important part of the NEW WORLD ORDER, DEMOCRATIC PARTY, and JOE BIDEN AGENDA, with the undying support of Social Media and Mainstream Media lies, propaganda, and indoctrination, the plan is to continue to keep it in the forefront for two reasons: appease liberal women, and more importantly, deflect from other issues of vastly more significance that the NEW WORLD ORDER, DEMOCRATIC PARTY, and JOE BIDEN AGENDA are losing on, in 2024, which is basically everything else."

"America's Public Enemy #1 in the United States is drug abuse. In order to fight and defeat this enemy it is necessary to wage a new, all-out offensive. ...This will be a world-wide-offensive..."
-President Richard M. Nixon 1971

"I wasn't alive when Nixon said that, but I was well aware of it. It was amazing to watch how quickly Americans were willing to dismiss Nixon's warning. There are so many things going on in America in 2024 that it's tough to keep track of them, yet, when I think back to how the BIDEN ADMINISTRTION and Gavin Newsom, our Governor, were actually promoting drug use and abuse, it was hard to believe."

"ALL of it was by design, by the NEW WORLD ORDER. Their plan had always been, especially in 2024, to make America fight a bunch of wars on a bunch of fronts so that resources would be spread so thin that it would result in *NO* solutions. And one of their biggest coups was keeping Americans addicted to drugs. Drugs make people addicted to many things, with the actual drug only being one of them. Drugs, at all levels make people addicted to laziness, complacency, stupidity, ignorance, and most of all, which for the NEW WORLD ORDER was the *best of all*, obedience.

Drug users stupidly and defiantly believe that they are not addicts, but in truth, and by all definitions they are - even *functioning* addicts. But even they are only functioning at about 30% capacity and efficiency.

Why would anyone with an ounce of Common Sense, think, when the JOE BIDEN ADMINISTRATION, the GAVIN NEWSOM ADMINISTRATION, and any and all DEMOCRATIC PARTY–run governments are handing out free drugs, syringes, pills, and alcohol, that it is not purposeful. How insane is it that the narrative being played-out is that it is simply government being considerate and accommodating to all of its citizens, especially those who can't help themselves. Did anyone ever ask the next question, meaning, *How could they possibly help themselves if they are high on drugs 24/7?*

If government, at all levels, truly wanted to eliminate the drug problem, the solution is pretty rudimentary. All they would have to do is eliminate the drugs, and by default the drug problems would go away. But they don't want that."

"I remember how Fentanyl was overtaking the country back in 2024."

"Again, by design, and also taking it to the next level. The Drug Cartels of Mexico and other Central American and South American countries got all the help they needed from Joe Biden. He opened the Southern border and the Drug Cartels from all of these countries swarmed across the border. In 2024 they had a foothold in every state in America. The Chinese in 2024 did the same. And, per the plan, the BIDEN ADMINISTRATION kept up the same propaganda and lies that the border was secure. But what Americans didn't realize was that it *was* secure - just not for the United States. The BIDEN ADMINISTRATION was securing it by keeping it *open* to allow the Drug Cartels and Drug Traffickers to enter freely, knowing that they had a free pass to do whatever they wanted."

Traveler went on to explain that under the BIDEN ADMINISTRATION, America suffered:

- 106,699 drug-overdose deaths in 2021.
- 107,941 drug-overdose deaths in 2022.

"And then the BIDEN ADMINISTRATON proudly *bragged* that the number of drug-overdose deaths had decreased in 2023 to 107,533. Truth be known, it hadn't. 2024 topped them all, but the BIDEN ADMINISTRATION, in typical form, fudged the numbers to make it look like the problem had leveled-off, which was meant to look like a victory. It was pretty much like their propaganda on Inflation."

"What do you think the answer is?"

"The answer is, recognizing the real problem. The problem was Joe Biden. The problem was that Joe Biden was the pawn of the NEW WORLD ORDER. The problem was that they didn't care. They weren't in charge to care, they were in charge to help the problem continue to be a problem, and drain resources to make it look like they were trying. It also played directly into the homeless problem. NEWSOM allocated 24 BILLION DOLLARS to fight homelessness. In 2024, clearly recognizing the homeless problem in California had gotten worse, someone finally asked, "Where exactly did the money go? Where is the accounting?" As quickly as it was asked, it was forgotten."

"The problems are clear enough. But, what is the answer?"

"For starters, Americans need to stop being willing to turn the other cheek; for Americans to stop, always wanting to play nice; for

Americans to stop being suckers. And much of that is evidenced by what we know already happened in 2024. The NEW WORLD ORDER stayed in power and by 2038, Planet Earth was simply another barren wasteland like the other planets in the Solar System.

With that said, answers are nothing more than words. However, actions speaks louder than words. If you are successful in getting the NEW WORLD ORDER *out* of the White House in 2024, meaning any candidate of the DEMOCRATIC PARTY, including the Closer, and Donald Trump gets elected, you will have a voice to help him take the following ACTIONS:

- Officially declare DRUGS a threat to American sovereignty.

- Officially, and legally, declare war on all Drug Cartels, and their *soldiers/military,* meaning anyone and everyone involved in the cultivating, manufacture, distribution, and selling of any illegal and illicit DRUGS.

- Announce to the world, that the United States of America will be taking the WAR ON DRUGS to foreign soils if necessary. And if those countries don't help, then those countries will be on the United States list of undesirables, and subject to bone-crushing sanctions.

- Start using the US Military, specifically all divisions that have *Navy Seal Team*-types of units to take-down, destroy, arrest, or even kill, if met with deadly-force-resistance, any and all who are on American soil. Once this is done, every police force in the United States will be on-board to help.

To repeat myself for the umpteenth time - If the NEW WORLD ORDER and the DEMOCRATIC PARTY keep the White House in 2024, it is

GAME OVER for the United States of America, and the entire WORLD shortly thereafter."

"Big Tech and Social Media, without question, are the strongarm branches of NEW WORLD ORDER, DEMOCRATIC PARTY, and JOE BIDEN AGENDA for the dissemination of lies, propaganda, and indoctrination. Remember, on March 9, 2022, *without* the approval of Congress, and behind closed doors, using Executive Authority and Order 14067, Section 4, Joe Biden gave the federal government, and more specifically *his* federal government legal surveillance authority over all citizens, their bank accounts and purchases. And how did the NEW WORLD ORDER, DEMOCRATIC PARTY, and Joe Biden accomplish this? By using the information gained from Social Media databases, tweets, emails, and texts.

And of course, the NEW WORLD ORDER, DEMOCRATIC PARTY, and Joe Biden know this, and managed to prevent the Republicans from stopping it, using the same outlets to fend off the Republican efforts to stop it. The Republicans never learned to do what the NEW WORLD ORDER, DEMOCRATIC PARTY, and JOE BIDEN ADMINISTRATION did, and that was to keep pounding away, day after day, to rein-in the Media sites by taking their protections away under Section 230 US Code 47. But, going back to the Republicans in Congress- They're wimps, and the NEW WORLD ORDER knows it, and exploits it."

"So, what do I do about it?"

"Nothing. Don't waste any time or effort on trying to change anything with Big Tech and Social Media sites. It would be a waste of your time, as the NEW WORLD ORDER controls all of them. And to make matters worse, the NEW WORLD ORDER also owns and controls the majority of DEMOCRATIC PARTY Congressmen and Senators. That is why *Bill* after *Bill* gets proposed to reign-in the BIG TECH and Social Media sites and take away their federal protections, and why none of them get passed. Why would Democrats pass something that would undermine their power?

"You mean I'm supposed to ignore them?"

"You can't ignore them, realistically, but you don't have the time, money, power, or backing to go on a full attack. That will have to wait until after the election. If GOOD wins, you'll have a chance. If EVIL wins, it won't matter. Remember, by EVIL winning, all of the Social Media sites will be gone soon enough anyway. In the end it will be like they committed suicide by supporting EVIL."

"The secret of freedom lies in educating people, whereas the secret of tyranny is in keeping them ignorant."
-Maximilien Robespierre

"Makes sense, doesn't it? Educated people ask questions, and uneducated people don't. Educated people question authority, and uneducated people don't. Educated people want to think for themselves, and uneducated people want the government to do the thinking for them, or should I say, *need* the government to do the thinking for them. It sort of goes hand-in-hand with the benefits of a country being run as a Meritocracy.

And, how have the NEW WORLD ORDER, DEMOCRATIC PARTY, and JOE BIDEN ADMINISTRATION been systematically making America less educated?

- By *NOT* focusing on Reading, Writing, and Arithmetic in public schools.

- By using the COVID pandemic to shut down schools and education.

- By using the teacher's unions, and teachers to promote DEI, the trans-agenda, anti-whiteness, anti-Judaism, anti-Asian, and anti-everything-and-anything that doesn't adhere to the NEW WORLD ORDER, DEMOCRATIC PARTY, and JOE BIDEN AGENDA.

- By flooding our public schools and school grounds with illegals so that the schools have to shut down.

By also, in some cities, flooding public schools with non-English speaking students so that the entire education system is shut down, making Americans less educated and more prone in later years to accepting propaganda and lies."

"Make no mistake about it, the followers of the NEW WORLD ORDER are Liberals, which by definition means they are void of having simple Logic. The reason is fairly simple - Logic requires thought and reasoning, and Liberals have been conditioned for far too long to let someone else do the thinking for them. Logic is a concept so foreign to Liberals that the mere mention of the word completely blocks the synapses of their brains.

Closing schools for the reasons they used was a perfect example of Illogicalness. The general consensus among logical conservatives, especially in the medical community, was that children were not any more vulnerable to COVID than they were to the common cold. Therefore, shutting down the schools was not necessary. Secondly, and because of their *invulnerability* to COVID, children didn't need to take the untested faux-vaccine. But the lies, propaganda and indoctrination machine of the NEW WORLD ORDER, the DEMOCRATIC PARTY, the WHO, the CDC, BIG PHARMA, and all Social Media sites controlled by them, pushed the untested vaccine to the limits.

The point of all this is that the NEW WORLD ORDER, et al, did everything to harm the children of the world with all of the lies, propaganda, and indoctrination, promoting the false narrative that protection of the children meant the necessity of closing the schools, and ultimately was somehow in everyone's best interests. Control the narrative, and feed the propaganda. It's what the NEW WORLD ORDER did best.

If you want further confirmation of doing the opposite of what should be done for the children of the world, just look at the Office of the Stoogeon General in California in 2024. Are you familiar with the concept of Adverse Childhood Experiences (ACEs)?"

"No."

"I'm going to try and keep this short, as my point is to further show how the NEW WORLD ORDER was telling those willing to listen to them that what they were doing was GOOD, when, in fact, they did everything in their power to insure that the outcome was EVIL. The list of ACEs include: verbal/emotional abuse, physical abuse, sexual abuse, household dysfunction which can also be in the form of a parent being incarcerated, parental separation, parental divorce. All of these experiences, or abuses, are what shattered the chances for millions of children to experience a normal childhood.

The purpose of identifying these things was to help people who had suffered these abuses change their life around, as adults, and eliminate the abuses from happening when the children are growing up. All of these abuses, eventually, will be the underlying causes of alcoholism, drug abuse, depression, sleep disorders, and violence in all forms, including rape, murder, and suicide.

Just one of these abuses can eventually trigger one or more of the resultant abuses upon others. As expected, it gets exponentially worse as the number of abuses occur. Now go back and look at the list of abuses and tell me how many apply to a child whose parents, and/or teachers, think the child needs gender dysphoria counseling, puberty blockers, hormones, breast implants, and eventually castration and hysterectomies.

Given enough time, all ten ACEs will infect the brain of the child having this kind of abuse forced upon them. What chance will they have for a normal life? And as you personally saw, suicide rates in 2024 were almost five times what they were when you were born."

"I think I understand what you're getting at, so let me verbalize it, for confirmation. The NEW WORLD ORDER, with the help of the DEMOCRATIC PARTY, the BIDEN ADMINISTRATION, the CDC, the WORLD HEALTH ORGANIZATION, BIG PHARMA, and the BIDEN JUSTICE DEPARTMENT, claim that their intent is to protect children who really don't need protecting, and by doing so are actually doing irreparable harm to the children."

"I couldn't have said it better, myself... One more thing. Governor Newsom appointed Diana Ramos to be California Stoogeon General for one reason and one reason only, and that was because her resume read like the perfect NEW WORLD ORDER devotee. And for the record- straight to HELL.

"Amen."

"America will never be destroyed from the outside. If we falter and lose our freedoms, it will be because we destroyed ourselves."
-Abraham Lincoln

"The world had a lot of great people, as some of the quotes I have provided clearly shone. Nonetheless, all, by 2024 had been ignored. Mr. Lincoln was clearly a visionary when it pertained to America, and it was sad to watch the prediction unfold."

"It's not something that anyone with an ounce of Common Sense would disagree with."

"Unfortunately, you're dealing with the NEW WORLD ORDER and the DEMOCRATIC PARTY, so Common Sense doesn't apply. To be more specific to the warning, if you want to destroy a country, start with destroying the family unit. And the NEW WORLD ORDER, DEMOCRATIC PARTY, and JOE BIDEN ADMINISTRATION certainly did it by using DIVERSITY, EQUITY, INCLUSION, and CRITICAL RACE THEORY to do it.

DEI and CRITICAL RACE THEORY are both components of EVIL, and a major contributor to the propaganda, lies, and indoctrination theme of the NEW WORLD ORDER, DEMOCRATIC PARTY, and JOE BIDEN agenda. But there is a deeper and darker side to implementation of DEI and CRITICAL RACE THEORY. By dividing the country into smaller groups, and convincing each group that they are both special and oppressed, simultaneously, you can control them more easily. If the groups are unified, they are stronger, and less likely to be controlled.

Already, in 2024, the *melting pot* portrayal of America had disintegrated in favor of a multi-burner stove-top version, with every ethnicity coming into America and settling with *their own*, which was a component of DEI and CRITICAL RACE THEORY that everyone ignored. In generations past, they would go to the enclaves of immigrant countrymen and then eventually assimilate into the *American* culture. Not anymore. Los Angeles was ten different cities in one, and there were government-made signs on every freeway and major city street to prove it."

"You know, I think you're right. You're a million times smarter than most."

"With that acknowledgement, please let me continue. The GOOD in America, meaning anyone who opposes the NEW WORLD ORDER, DEMOCRATIC PARTY, and JOE BIDEN ADMINISTRATION, recognize just how harmful DEI and CRITICAL RACE THEORY are, especially to young children. The NEW WORLD ORDER, DEMOCRATIC PARTY, and JOE BIDEN agenda is to convince children at a very young age that White is Bad and most other colors are Good. They want to divide schoolrooms by race and tell the non-whites that they are not as good as the whites and therefore must hate whites. They also teach the students that Meritocracy and Education are Bad, but if you think that being a boy is better than being a girl because your brothers play baseball in the street and won't let the girls play, then take puberty blockers, have your breasts removed, follow it up with a hysterectomy, become a boy, and then you can play with them."

"That's so sick."

"Well, as was clearly the byproduct of their actions, if the kids weren't sick before the NEW WORLD ORDER got a hold of them, they certainly were shortly thereafter, both physically and mentally.

There are *boys* and *girls*, which the NEW WORLD ORDER, DEMOCRATIC PARTY, and JOE BIDEN ADMINISTRATION don't want anyone to say or recognize anymore. Public School teachers and educators, without parental consent questioned a First Grader about their sexual identity, as if a First Grader can even comprehend what that means. But they did it anyway, and then used the confused answers of the children to enact a plan whereby girls as young as eight years were given hysterectomies and boys of the same age were castrated."

"I heard it was happening and knew it was happening, but I was helpless to try and stop it."

"I know. The Critical Race Theory infusion into the public schools, which the Teacher's Unions denied was happening was a prime example of their indoctrination plan for children. All that anyone had to do was sit back and observe any First-Grade classroom in America. Children, as a rule, don't recognize the differences or question the differences of their classmates, ever. They are all equal and the same at that age. But the NEW WORLD ORDER, DEMOCRATIC PARTY, and JOE BIDEN AGENDA decided that the world could not have *naturally occurring* diversity, and harmony. What is better is to teach Critical Race Theory, and by so doing go back three hundred years and drag up commonplace class distinctions, bigotry, and even hate, so that the country divides the children at this young and vulnerable age, and then that will start to tear down the nuclear family.

What kind of country had America become where teachers and educators believed that children are no longer their *parents'* children after they step into a classroom in a public school? Since the beginning of time, children were born and raised by GOOD parents, allowed to play in a world of GOOD, and live a life of GOOD. But in 2021, with Joe Biden and the NEW WORLD ORDER getting into the White House, once the children stepped onto public school property they were catapulted into the realm of EVIL, where education became second to manipulation and indoctrination by the NEW WORLD ORDER, the DEMOCRATIC PARTY, and JOE BIDEN agenda.

Yet, the NEW WORLD ORDER, DEMOCRATIC PARTY, and JOE BIDEN ADMINISTRATION will boldly say that parents who question these practices and condemn these practices, are terrorists. The NEW WORLD ORDER, DEMOCRATIC PARTY, and Joe Biden media affiliates, support this practice and do everything in their power through continual lies, propaganda, and indoctrination, to make the voices of the NEW WORLD ORDER, DEMOCRATIC PARTY, and JOE BIDEN ADMINSTRATION stronger, and that of GOOD parents, weaker. *That,* in its purest form is Domestic Terrorism."

"What I found interesting about Artificial Intelligence was that it had been around, technically, since the first microchip was invented. Before you knew it, the first generation of microchips was inventing the second generation of microchips by interfacing with the "mother" boards of computers that were using, analyzing, and integrating the data to advance the intelligence of machines."

"It was really never clear how much the robots of my time were actually thinking."

"They were actually utilizing *Critical Thinking*, which by definition is having the ability to *analyze* data and then form a judgement as to what direction should be taken going forward. Think of it like a chess game, which was one of the first tests of a computer to *think*. From the move of the first pawn the computer was immediately considering and analyzing hundreds of thousands of possibilities of what its response move could be, and then analyzing what its opponent's next move would be. At some point, the computer would decide from what *could* be, to what *should* be, the computer's move. Now keep in mind that if a computer and Grand Master were to play, after the game the computer could be fed the data from every move on the part of the Grand Master, to the point where eventually the Grand Master would not have the mental capacity to beat the computer. Artificial Intelligence in 2024 was still in its infancy. By 2032 it was a million times faster and smarter, for lack of a better word, and able to do the bidding of the NEW WORLD ORDER by not possessing the ability to know or care the what or why of that which was being demanded of it. A perfect example was when the NEW WORLD ORDER directed their AI computers to find a vulnerable doorway into the Chinese genome. The morality of such a request, as it was a machine, was never an issue."

"It was almost as if they were trying to hide what AI could actually do."

"Most definitely they were. They knew the potential and downplayed it. There is also a second example of AI. It was Joe Biden, himself. From the moment he agreed to the terms of the NEW WORLD ORDER to just be a shill for their agenda, they agreed to give him something that he was already too braindead to recognize that he didn't have- Intelligence. For their promise to fulfill a dream of his, that he could have never gotten on his own, meaning the Presidency, they agreed to use every drug they knew of to keep him coherent enough to know what day it was, even if having to use a teleprompter to remind him. That was the *real* Artificial Intelligence.

"This is when I know I'm not a real angel yet, because I want to laugh and still can."

"Here's an opportunity to discuss one of the strongest allies of the NEW WORLD ORDER- The WORLD HEALTH ORGANIZATION (WHO), which wasn't really an ally but an attached arm of the NEW WORLD ORDER that did it's bidding in every way, shape, and form."

"From everything I have learned, I know that the WORLD HEALTH ORGANIZATION was *all-in* when it came to COVID and the vaccine."

"And you would be 100% accurate. The NEW WORLD ORDER was behind it all, with the help of BIG PHARMA, the UNITED NATIONS, and the WORLD HEALTH ORGANIZATION. Subsequently they had every country in the world under their thumb. It goes back to all of the components of their ability to CONTROL everything; in effect enforcing their basic rule to never let anyone hear the truth or know the truth... And at all cost, never let the truth get out.

What the NEW WORLD ORDER did with COVID was typical. They, in collusion with BIG PHARMA, created an untested vaccine that by legal definition wasn't a vaccine, and then got the WORLD HEALTH ORGANIZATION, the CDC, and the BIDEN ADMINISTRATION to change the definition to make the non-vaccine a vaccine, under the new definition. Then they released it, having never tested it, to see if the general public would accept it. They created fear by propaganda that it would be the end of the world is everyone didn't fall into line to get faux-vaccinated, and then they shut down the country to keep the fear at the forefront of the conversation and to be the basis for a country-wide shut-down on all fronts. And it worked.

An official who served on the CDC Advisory Committee on Immunization during the Obama administration was captured on video calling for genocide against white people in America in order to eliminate those who resisted vaccines. And then there was this:

"We flew the aeroplane while we were still building it. We got creative- we couldn't wait for data, we had to do so much at risk."
- Kathrin Jansen, Pfizer vaccine R&D

Another example of Mass Formation Psychosis."

"Looking back, I remember that people like Bill Gates were publicly welcoming a future pandemic to reduce the world population."

"And then the NEW WORLD ORDER propaganda machine did everything in its power to deny access to videos of him saying it, and replaced it with an onslaught of videos by Bill Gates saying that we need to prepare for the next pandemic and how to avoid it.

More importantly, everyone ignored him when he said that all should put their faith in the WORLD HEALTH ORGANIZATION, the GLOBAL HEALTH EMERGENCY CORPS, the GLOBAL EPIDEMIC RESPONSE & MOBILIZATION (GERM) team, and for good measure, BIG PHARMA."

"I could never figure out how Bill Gates emerged as such an authority on pandemics."

"Bill Gates was a perfect candidate to sit at the high-table of the NEW WORLD ORDER. He was smart, rich, successful, had control over much of what the world saw and heard, and was a narcissist of the highest order, meaning he thought he knew what was best for everyone else. People listened to him, which was their biggest mistake. All of the agencies he was promoting were controlled by the NEW WORLD ORDER."

"I remember when the WORLD HEALTH ORGANIZATION was pushing total control over world political policies, using a future pandemic as their bait to get the control"

"We talked about this a little bit earlier, but at the time you are going back, meaning 2024, they are making their final plea to the mindless, which includes plenty of muted conservatives, to allow them full control at the World Health Assembly. Using the same ploy that they used with the Gruesome Newsom recall, of showing you what happened and telling you it was something else; the same tactic was utilized by offering the promise of "pandemic preparedness," to try and get the masses behind their scheme. The Children's Health Defense, of your time, clearly warned everyone, of all of this. They pointed out that the WHO, by passing their proposal, would:

- Change IHR (International Health Regulations) recommendations from 'non-binding' to legally binding, meaning all member countries must comply.

- Create requirements for health documents that could be used to restrict access and travel as the WHO sees fit.

- Require surveillance of online information and censorship of information deemed "Misinformation."

- Coerce extreme lockdown measures, including creating quarantine of suspect travelers, preferable in facilities away from the point of entry, "aka quarantine camps, seen during the COVID-19 pandemic in China and elsewhere.

- Allow the WHO to declare an emergency at will.

- Require member nations to use certain "relevant health products like vaccines, drugs, etc., while others are prohibited during emergencies."

"Why would anyone agree to this? Even I was one of those who said we should have never gotten on board with the WHO."

"It was just another checkmark on the need-to-do list of the NEW WORLD ORDER, meaning having the United States on board. There was an attempt to get out. The WHO Withdrawal Act, HR79, was introduced in the U.S. House, but the NEW WORLD ORDER and BIDEN ADMINISTRATION quashed it."

"They did everything *to us* that they said they were trying to protect us from."

"The NEW WORLD ORDER was determined, but there was a glimmer of hope in June 2024, when numerous organizations like the Children's Health Defense, stopped the WHO in its tracks. Unfortunately it was short-lived, as days after the election was over and the NEW WORLD ORDER was in full control, it was brought back up and passed. In the end, the WHO and the NEW WORLD ORDER got their way.

Boldly. They gave the world their playbook for the final takedown, and everyone agreed to it. Suckers to the end. Two-hundred and fifty-four years in the planning, and less than five years to finally carry it out."

"And I lived to see it."

"And died as a result. Punish the righteous and reward the wicked. The NEW WORLD ORDER knew from Day 1 that Biden would never make it to the 2024 election. But they didn't care. Biden's role was to agree to everything they were willing to do to get him elected, and that was enough for Biden. The biggest problem came when Biden started to believe that he was actually the President of the United States. So, they left him alone to wallow in his delusional presidency until they were ready to initiate the next phase, and the final phase of their plan to destroy the United States of America once and for all, by getting rid of Biden, Ha-Ha Harris, and bringing in the *Closer* to end it all.

"The NEW WORLD ORDER had been doing everything in its power to convince everyone in the Free World that if they we're going to compete with China, that they must *be* like China, and to compete with China on the world stage the Free World must adopt a digital Currency going forward. In 2022 the Digital currency crash that bilked millions from investors was a well-forged plan for the NEW WORLD ORDER to point out the fraud that caused the crash, and then say that there needed to be new rules going forward to prevent it from happening again. Again, Bait and Switch. When many of the cryptocurrencies crashed in 2022, notice that Bitcoin didn't, and then ask yourself, *why not*? Because China owned most of it.

When Biden is gone in October 2024, the Closer will enact Trump policies on the border, oil drilling and exploration, with the message being, "Why does anyone need Trump?" It was a rallying cry of the NEW WORLD ORDER and the DEMOCRATIC PARTY to use in pointing out that the sudden surge in popularity of the new candidate had brought the race to a point where it was too close to call, meaning that with a little ala 2020 sleaze-tactics, the election again went to the NEW WORLD ORDER candidate. Game over!

"Going back as far as Dec 2022, the NEW WORLD ORDER was making its move. The food supply of Europe was under direct assault via multiple schemes that were designed to end affordable food. At the same time, electricity was becoming unaffordable for businesses and residential households alike. Germany was ordering farmers to slash nitrogen fertilizer usage, a move that resulted in massive crop losses leading to food scarcity, inflation and famine. This was all being done on purpose.

The real goal, of course, was genocide against humanity. They called it Global Depopulation. Thousands of farms were taken over or shut down by governments in Europe, and it was all done in the name of "climate science."

Next they wanted everyone to believe that everybody had to be locked down to prevent the spread of Covid. Obviously that was all false. As a matter of fact the opposite was true. Locking down senior citizens in a single location made the disease spread faster. Then they wanted everyone to believe that respirators were needed for anyone who had Covid. Another lie.

With the help of the BIDEN ADMINISTRATION, oil drilling was stopped, and the same for natural gas, which the United States had enough of, underground, to heat and power the USA for the next 80 years. During that time the USA could have continued to develop and utilize cleaner forms of energy. But the NEW WORLD ORDER saw no need for any of this because they were not preparing to help- they were preparing to destroy."

"One of the most used statements of Mankind was, *If I only knew then, what I know now.*"

Almost to the point of total embarrassment, Chelsea responded, "That certainly applies to me, in a very big way."

Traveler was well aware of the obviousness of her regret at having to admit it. Nonetheless, Traveler continued with his teachings, to keep Chelsea engaged. "I'm specifically referring to knowing the *Real Joe Biden*, whose political career reeked of duplicity, exaggerations, desperation, and genuine ignorance.

By comparison, all one has to do is look to the words of someone who actually dealt with Joe Biden; a man who by most accounts was considered the Greatest American President of the Modern era - Ronald Reagan. Though he was a bit before your time, most Americans, on both sides of the aisle, were impressed with the Common-Sense approach to the needs of America by President Ronald Reagan.

"Freedom is never more than one generation away from extinction. We didn't pass it to our children in the bloodstream. It must be fought for, protected, and handed-on for them to do the same, or one day we will spend our sunset years telling our children and our children's children what it was once like in the United States where men were free."

"My parents absolutely loved Ronald Reagan. They also liked his *Peace through Strength* approach to the sovereignty of America."

"And those words echoed through the future generations and served as the motto of protection for the United States under most presidents. But that abruptly ended in 2021, on Day 1 of the Biden Presidency. It was immediately evident that the *opposite* of Ronald Reagan was Joe Biden. By comparison, BIDEN was weak, clueless, and ineffectual, except on the EVIL scale, which as you now know were the primary traits needed for him to be the puppet of the NEW WORLD ORDER. I know it to be true that in the higher rankings of the NEW WORLD ORDER they jokingly referred to him as *Brain Dead Joe*.

It had always been the case with Joe Biden. Going back to his infancy in the Senate, thinking he was going to make points as a Junior-Senator-running-for-President, Brain Dead Joe stated, when Reagan stood in front of Berlin's Brandenburg Gate and said, 'Mr. Gorbachev, tear down this wall!', that Reagan should have never dared to make such a demand.

Obviously Biden was wrong about criticizing Reagan, but he never learned from any of his mistakes as he was about 99% *wrong* on everything he ever said or did in his thirty-six years in the Senate, paving the way for former CIA Director and Defense Secretary Robert Gates, who served under several presidents from both political parties, to famously say:

'that Biden had been wrong about "nearly every major foreign policy and national security issue over the past four decades.'"

To further the narrative about Biden's shortcomings, an excerpt from Reagan's personal diary recalled:

'A liberal friend of mine told me within this past year that Biden is a "purely transactional" politician. That's what makes demagoguery come so easily to him: His only conviction is that he should be president, so he'll say whatever it takes to get there. And on... the many times he is wrong, well, he'll just discard his demagoguery on that issue and move on to the next one.'

Take note that a *Liberal* said that! Keep in mind that the Liberal's assessment, coupled with Biden's other mental flaws are what made him the perfect puppet for the NEW WORLD ORDER's plans. *Brain Dead Joe,* in a last-ditch-effort to be President of the United States, agreed to do anything to get there, just as Ronald Reagan's friend had said.

If you want to take the discussion to the next level, go to Google in 2024, and see their definition of *demagogue.*

Demagogue - a political leader who seeks support by appealing to the desires and prejudices of ordinary people rather than by using rational argument.

"Unfortunately, in 2024 there were still tens of millions who ignored the obviousness of Joe Biden the demagogue, in favor of the propaganda and lies of the NEW WORLD ORDER that did everything in their power to shield and protect him from any questions that would have revealed the *Real Joe Biden.*"

"Let me guess- the NEW WORLD ORDER didn't want anyone to hear the truth, know the truth, or let the truth get out."

"You're definitely catching on."

"Before I go, I'm curious about one more person. Hunter Biden."

"You know, I could fill a laptop with ten gigabytes of information on Hunter Biden, and none of it would be good. So, let me leave you with a few quick facts, and one, gigantic ending thought.

- Joe Biden became Vice President in 2009.
- Hunter Biden suddenly and mysteriously partnered with a Shanghai investment group to purchase a Michigan based auto parts manufacturer.
- One year later, Hunter was discharged from the Naval Reserves after testing positive for cocaine. Keep in mind that he had a cocaine problem going back to the 1980s.
- The very same year, Hunter joined the Board of Burisma, a Ukrainian energy company that was already under investigation for corruption, and neither Joe Biden or Barack Obama questioned it.
- Joe Biden's other son, Beau, died of cancer and Hunter used it as an excuse to relapse into alcohol addiction.
- The very next year, 2016, Hunter also got addicted to crack cocaine.
- Shortly thereafter, in 2017, he got into a romantic relationship with his brother's widow, Hallie. And then she also started using crack cocaine with him.
- In August 2018, Hunter had a child out of wedlock with a different woman, with whom he had an affair while romantically involved with his brother's widow.
- Hunter perjured himself on a federal handgun purchase form, indicating he was not a drug user.
- Had to be legally forced to pay alimony and child support
- The same year, 2018, Hunter left his laptop at a repair shop, that was filled with hundreds of photos of him using drugs and being with prostitutes.

- In 2019 he met another woman, and married her 6 days later."

"Was that all of it? I honestly don't remember."

"Not even close to all of it. Those are just a few of the highlights. Hunter Biden never denied any of it because he couldn't, and more importantly never showed any remorse, embarrassment, or contrition, for any of it.

And Joe Biden, the man who was President of the United States and thought he should have been reelected was publicly and excitedly *proud* of a decadent, immoral, corrupt, and degenerate son, believing that all Americans should have also been *proud* of him. Even after Hunter's 3-count felony conviction in 2024 for lying on a federal ATF gun-purchase form, Joe Biden, again was saying he was *proud* of Hunter.

Man had always held onto the principle of leading by example, and if being proud of Hunter, and sharing in the wealth that Hunter brought into the family from foreign countries is an example of true leadership, then the United States was in big trouble even without the NEW WORLD ORDER."

"In spite of his mental deficiency, I'm still a little surprised that God gave Joe Biden a pass."

"Yes, he did. But for the record, not Hunter."

Chelsea finalized her thoughts on the matter Scripture. "...for whatsoever a man soweth, that shall he also reap."

Traveler smiled in approval. "Amen. However, don't discount the words of one of your Founding Fathers, who, not knowing at the time that he would be describing what would be the followers of a cult that was founded while he was alive, meaning leftist minions of the NEW WORLD ORDER, or even the proud son of a sitting President."

*"We are all born ignorant, but one must work
hard to remain stupid."*

— *Benjamin Franklin*

"You know I read minds, so I'll skip the question and go right to the answer. You're scared to death."

"There's no denying it."

"Are you more afraid of the fight, or the risk of failure and what it means for the world?"

"As you have already surmised, both. I'm going back in June 2024, and I am well aware that Donald Trump had just been convicted in that sham trial in New York. If the NEW WORLD ORDER, the JOE BIDEN ADMINISTRATION, and the DEPARTMENT OF JUSTICE could carry out that type of illegal prosecution and get away with it, I'm scared what they'll try with me."

"If anything, Donald Trump should be your inspiration. They were *never* able to break him. He showed the type of courage and fortitude that I rarely saw in anyone, and I have seen all of them. I know you're big on quotes, so let me tell you one that should also be your encouragement to do your best in the face of all diversity that you will meet. It also is a great example of what drives Donald Trump. It comes from the movie, *Rocky Balboa,* with Sylvester Stallone, another man of great courage and fortitude who became a movie star, in spite of all that was thrown against him.

'Let me tell you something you already know. The world ain't all sunshine and rainbows. It's a very mean and nasty place and I don't care how tough you are. It will beat you to your knees and keep you there permanently if you let it. You, me, or nobody is gonna hit as hard as life. But it ain't about how hard ya hit. It's about how hard you can get hit and keep moving forward. How much you can take and keep moving forward. That's how winning is done!'

Chelsea thought about the quote, and was shaking her head in approval. "Then, Rocky it is. But I'm still hoping you can give me a heads-up about any particulars, meaning what I'll be up against."

"No particulars are available. Whatever happens is *going* to happen, and God is the only one who knows. The simplest answer is, everything. Every arm of the NEW WORLD ORDER will, in a collective effort, try to silence you at all cost. You are up against decades of propaganda, mind control, stupidity, ignorance and everything else that the NEW WORLD ORDER has managed to use to bring half of the United States into submission to their messaging. The result is that the NEW WORLD ORDER has successfully convinced these people that the forces of GOOD are lying, and the forces of EVIL are telling the truth, when, as anyone who managed to keep their free will and common sense knows, is the opposite of truth and reality.

For starters, they will see this book as a threat to their very existence, and therefore must try to discredit you and the book itself, saying it's a conspiracy theory fantasy. But you have to figure out how to counter their attacks, because it will be news, and you'll get enough attention to state your case. But one defense you might have, which will help to make sales and create awareness is to point out that writers like Jules Vern, Aldous Huxley, H.G. Wells, and Ray Bradbury, wrote books with seemingly fantastical predictions, and though categorically fiction in the times they were written, eventually all of it came true in one form or another. Then they will try to stop the book from being published, using the reason that it is seditious, which technically would be another NEW WORLD ORDER lie, as it is anti-seditious. Unquestionably, this journey will test your character and strength to the limits."

"I was looking for encouragement."

"And Donald Trump and Rocky will give it to you. If you're looking for something a little more to your liking, try this...

> The Lord is my rock, and my fortress, and my deliverer:
> my God, my strength, in whom I will trust.
> *Psalm 18:2*

Chelsea was visibly pleased that Traveler had made the attempt to give her strength and support from her comfort zone, meaning the Bible.

"Thank you for that."

"You're welcome. And, here's your book, in paperback format, to submit to the publisher."

"Chelsea looked at the book and flipped through the pages."

"But I never said anything about the cover, or anything."

"You didn't have to. Remember?"

Chelsea laughed. "Will I see you again?"

"Someday. But I'll be there, watching."

"From the wings?"

"Exactly."

"Any final world of encouragement?"

"You asked God, *Where Was Your Wrath When We Needed It?* Maybe you're it! Give 'em Hell, Angela."

Angela Di Paradiso arrived on Earth in June 2024, just as she had planned. She self-published her book and set about getting copies of the book to people that she was hoping would help promote it. Two months after the first book was published, the book had sold enough copies to put her onto the NY Times Bestseller List, though the NEW WORLD ORDER saw to it that it never happened. CENSORSHIP was the order of the day from the NEW WORLD ORDER.

But conservatives embraced her and helped to get the book out to the masses, to let the *People* decide for themselves what should be the best course of action.

One month before the November 5, 2024 Presidential election, Angela was asked to be the guest speaker at a rally for Donald Trump. It was her final speech, and only public speech before the election.

"Thank you... I appreciate you having me here today, and I am very happy and proud that I managed to get the attention of a lot of different people from around the world because of a book I wrote, titled <u>Where Was Your Wrath When We Needed It?</u>

But before I continue, I would like to clear up a small mystery and confirm that my name, Angela Di Paradiso, is absolutely my God-given name."

Hoping all were aware that her name, Angela Di Paradiso, translated to Angel of Heaven, she continued her speech.

"We all have purpose, but the question is, will we recognize what that purpose is, and will we act on it? Will we do our best to give our best? Will we give our best, to, in the end get the best? Do we have what it takes to accomplish this? I can assure you that the test to find out is upon us, as the forces of EVIL are gaining strength and momentum to take away our God-given right to think for ourselves and guide ourselves to do what is right for ourselves, our families, our countries, our religions, and the world as we have known it.

When I sat down to write the book, the most important message that I wanted to convey is that we, the Human Race, are in the fight of our lives. We are in a war of GOOD vs. EVIL, and unfortunately, EVIL is winning. As I did more and more research I was actually scaring myself at the reality of just how evil, EVIL really is. So, I made it a point to put into the book all that I had found out, with the promise to myself that I would not lie or exaggerate. Then I discovered that I wouldn't have had to, as the truth of the NEW WORLD ORDER and its plan for world domination has been publicly expressed by the NEW WORLD ORDER, itself, and all of its subsidiaries, on many occasions. It is as real as it gets. But I am also of the opinion that you should never take my word for anything as gospel.

Ronald Reagan famously said, *Trust but Verify*. Unfortunately, we are beyond trusting anyone or anything in this day and time, and especially as it relates to the 2024 presidential election. We must *Verify*, before we *Trust*. But I caution you, that if you don't do it soon you will never be able to, as "they," meaning the NEW WORLD ORDER and the DEMOCRATIC PARTY, are making every attempt to make it so you can't find out the truth about anything. They have already banned books from publication, denied conservative and religious information and viewpoints from Social Media sites, and as we have seen all too often this year, have been arresting people without cause to harass them, silence them, and intimidate the masses into cowering out of fear if they dare to speak out against them. This is the world we are currently living in. And it will only get worse if we don't stop them now, meaning in the November 5 election.

The sad part of this is that there are too many who have already submitted, and are committed to somehow believing the NEW WORLD ORDER's propaganda machine, that promises...well to be honest, I'm not sure what *it* promises. But it begs the question- If GOOD is the promise of freedom of thought and expression, freedom of religious choice and practice, free will to live as we choose, have relationships, marriage, children, grandchildren, to have friends and neighbors, to live where we want, travel when and where we want, what could the NEW WORLD ORDER and the DEMOCRATIC PARTY be promising to make people desire the *opposite* of GOOD? How is that possible? And yet, it is.

Earlier, I talked about purpose. Part One, for me, was to do the research and write the book. And though I have taken much criticism for even suggesting it, I know that in my heart, and in my soul, that I found my purpose, meaning to write the book and be here tonight. My purpose is to be God's earthly messenger, to share my thoughts, my visions, and my prayers for a better tomorrow, which can only be achieved by a unified effort of peoples of all religions and all countries who truly want to defeat EVIL in all of its forms.

I believe that my justification for everything was very clearly defined in my book, but I am also aware that a specific goal is often times better than a general one. I believe that our first, specific goal will be to win the Presidential Election this November 5. When you look at the forces of EVIL, namely the NEW WORLD ORDER and the DEMOCRATIC PARTY, it is glowingly clear that none of their policies will give us any of the freedoms that we have enjoyed since Man first walked on Earth. Over the past decade or so we have witnessed changes in every facet of our very existence, and in every corner of this planet. The forces of EVIL have been working effortlessly to control our lives on every level, to ultimately break us and leave us with no alternative but to surrender our free will at every turn, and submit to their iron-fisted rule. This would mean human suffering on a scale we have never witnessed before under their reign of terror. We are looking at Hell on Earth, if EVIL wins the election.

I am well aware that I, and my book, have been the target of the NEW WORLD ORDER, as they have been using the press and Social Media sites that they control to reinforce the propaganda that <u>Where Was Your Wrath When We Needed It?</u> is a wildly, disingenuous work of fiction, to quote their repetitive messaging. But to you, and to those who will listen, let me pose *this*, for you to use as a non-combative weapon to get *them* to listen to you.

I would say to anyone who refuses to believe the facts, as outlined in the book, or its message -

- *Is it possible that even 10% of what is written here could be true?* It's not likely that even the staunchest of the currently mind-controlled minions of the NEW WORLD ORDER and DEMOCRATIC PARTY could think that it wouldn't be possible.

- And then I would ask, *If 10% is possible, then the next question is,* which *10%?* If they hesitate, then the free-will and common sense that God gave them is beginning to reemerge. Which brings me to the next question that should be posed.

- *If 10% is true, but you don't know which 10%, then, obviously, it could be any 10%. And if it could be any 10%, then it could be two or more 10%'s, meaning that it could be 20%, 30%, 50%, or even 100%.*

The final question should be: Are you seriously willing to take that chance and ignore, even 10%? Are you willing to gamble your future, your family's future, the future of the United States of America, and the future of the entire world on anyone associated with the NEW WORLD ORDER, the DEMOCRATIC PARTY, and any and all of their Presidential or Vice-Presidential candidates?

It isn't often that we get a second chance to do anything. But when the opportunity arises we best not get it wrong a second time. We got it very wrong in 2020. 2024 can and should be our redemption.

As I stated over and over in the book, in the battle of GOOD vs. EVIL the first battleground is the United States of America. If we fall, the world falls.

I kept my messaging in the book to be about the battle of GOOD vs. EVIL. Nothing has changed, except that the time has come to call out EVIL, and make our final stand to support GOOD by defeating EVIL.

EVIL is the candidate that the NEW WORLD ORDER and the DEMOCRATIC PARTY has chosen. There is no other way to describe him.

Luckily we have a candidate for GOOD, who in his first term in office proved that he was GOOD on all levels, having had the best interests of all Americans in mind with every decision he made. I am talking about President Donald Trump.

But in spite of my undying support of President Trump, even I know that there are many out there who can't seem to see beyond the shroud of propaganda that the NEW WORLD ORDER and the DEMOCRATIC PARTY has draped, or even his personal character traits. As a result, even the consideration of voting for Donald Trump, for some, may not be an option, choosing instead to stay home and not vote for anyone, though believing that the threat of EVIL is greater than ever. So, to those non-supporters or uncommitted, I offer this.

There was a time in my life, meaning the primary season leading up to the 2016 election, that I was not a big fan of Donald Trump. But I voted for him anyway, especially in consideration of what the alternative was. In the final couple of months leading up to the election I found myself actively campaigning for the man that I hadn't liked only a few months before. And this is why - At some point after Donald Trump got the nomination, I had to take a closer look at the man that I knew I was going to vote for, which at that time was only going to be a vote for a man that was simply a much better, and obviously a much more honest and transparent candidate than Hillary Clinton.

What I discovered and came to accept, which is going to be a stretch for most anti-Trumpers, is to having a serious conversation with your conscience to start the process of thinking about what is best for you and the United States of America. And then, realize this-

Everything that you may not like about Donald Trump, meaning his personality, demeanor, and his willingness to go on the attack to defeat his enemies, or simply his political opponents, is what you should love and embrace about him as President of the United States. Especially now, because he has a record that proved in his first term in office that no one loves the United States of America more than Donald Trump. His love of country and its citizens is unparalleled, and no one will be more dedicated to protecting it.

If you were to take a serious look at what Donald Trump has endured over the past eight years, both as President of the United States and as a candidate leading up to the election on November 5, ask yourself this- What other person, politician, and American could have endured what he has endured, with the constant barrage of lies, propaganda, lawsuits, false indictments, court appearances, and gag orders, on a daily basis by the NEW WORLD ORDER, the DEMOCRATIC PARTY, the BIDEN ADMINISTRATION, the JUSTICE DEPARTMENT, and VARIOUS LOCAL AND STATE GOVERNMENTS? Who? I'll make this easy on you. No one. At least no one that we know of, as no one has ever been put to this test. But not only did Donald Trump survive, but he thrived in spite of it all.

Can you imagine Joe Biden having to deal with even one-one-hundredth of what they have put President Trump through? President Joe Biden would have gotten blown away into oblivion faster than a house of cards in a Category 5 hurricane if he had ever been attacked in the multiple ways that President Trump has, over the past eight years.

I can think of many words to describe the character of President Donald Trump: Strength, endurance, fortitude, honesty, transparency, loyalty, patriotic. The list goes on and on, and no one, not even the NEW WORLD ORDER and the DEMOCRATIC PARTY have been able to crush him, or his spirit. Have you seen Joe Biden show any of these traits? Ever?

What these traits do is make Donald Trump a beacon for GOOD, and our hope for the future of the United States of America.

Please get out and vote for GOOD. But don't stop there. Get out and spread the word to your family, friends, and neighbors. And get them to do the same."

Reinforce the fact that if GOOD wins, everyone wins.

But if EVIL wins, everyone loses.

Vote for GOOD.

Vote for Donald Trump.

and

GOD BLESS AMERICA !

"Give me liberty, or give me death"
-Nathan Hale 1776

www.ingramcontent.com/pod-product-compliance
Lightning Source LLC
Chambersburg PA
CBHW051739250726
48659CB00001B/156